D1300660

The Winter Queen

ROSALIND K. MARSHALL

THE
THE LIFE OF
WINTER
ELIZABETH OF BOHEMIA
QUEEN
1596–1662

EDINBURGH
Scottish National Portrait Gallery
MCMXCVIII

Published by the Trustees
of the National Galleries of Scotland
for the exhibition *The Winter Queen: The Life of Elizabeth of Bohemia*
held at the Scottish National Portrait Gallery, Edinburgh
10 July – 4 October 1998

ISBN 0 903598 79 5

Designed and typeset in Renard by Dalrymple
Printed by BAS Printers, Over Wallop

Front cover:
Elizabeth of Bohemia, 1622 by Michael van Mierevelt (detail)
[see plate 41]

Half title page:
Gilded silver goblet by H.C. Brechtel, 1641, presented
by Elizabeth to Leiden, where her children were educated.
A little figure of her stands on the lid.
Stedelijk Museum de Lakenhal, Leiden

Frontispiece:
Frederick, Elizabeth and their eldest son,
Prince Frederick Henry, medal, 1616
British Museum, London

SPONSORED BY

BAILLIE GIFFORD

Contents

THE WINTER QUEEN

Foreword

Elizabeth of Bohemia, so much better known to history as The Winter Queen, has ever been a popular and romantic figure; not least in her native Scotland. One of the three children of King James VI and I, Elizabeth married and fell in love with Frederick, the Elector Palatine. She was known in her lifetime as the Queen of Hearts. Living with their young family at Heidelberg Castle in the Rhineland, Frederick and Elizabeth were acknowledged as pillars of Protestantism at a time when Europe was bitterly divided by religious conflict. With trepidation, Frederick accepted the offer of the throne of Bohemia but, within months, he and his Queen were ousted from Prague in a coup d'état and lost Heidelberg and the Palatinate as well. Much of Elizabeth's subsequent life was spent in exile in The Hague, hoping in vain for her husband's return to Heidelberg while powerless to prevent the fall and execution of her brother King Charles I. At the end of her long life, Elizabeth was able to return once more to Britain to see her nephew King Charles II restored to her family's throne.

Dr Rosalind Marshall, Curator of the Portrait Archive of the Scottish National Portrait Gallery, is an internationally respected scholar who has published extensively on the Royal House of Stewart. In this book, the companion to an exhibition shown at the Scottish National Portrait Gallery in the summer of 1998, Dr Marshall explores the life and travels of The Winter Queen. Through the experiences of one remarkable woman, living at the centre of European politics, Dr Marshall has examined the conflicting pressures of personal interest and family loyalty.

Historically The Winter Queen has a further importance. Through her father King James and her grandmother Mary, Queen of Scots, Elizabeth was descended from King Duncan I, the ancestor of all subsequent Scottish Kings. From her grandfather, Lord Darnley as well as from her grandmother she could trace her descent from the Kings and Queens of England to before the Conquest. Elizabeth's daughter Sophia married the Elector of Hanover. Their son George became King of Great Britain in 1714 on the death of the last Stewart Monarch, Queen Anne. Princess Elizabeth, The Winter Queen, is therefore the crucial dynastic link between our present Royal Family and the Stewart, Tudor, Plantagenet and Norman kings of our history.

The National Galleries of Scotland would like to thank Her Majesty The Queen for lending paintings to the exhibition from the Royal Collection and allowing them to be illustrated in this book. We also acknowledge with gratitude the generosity of all our lenders, both public and private, who have shared their treasures with us. Lastly, the Scottish National Portrait Gallery is once again indebted to the generosity of our sponsor, Baillie Gifford. For many years the firm has been a staunch friend of the Portrait Gallery. We much appreciate their continuing and vital support.

TIMOTHY CLIFFORD
Director, National Galleries of Scotland

JAMES HOLLOWAY
Keeper, Scottish National Portrait Gallery

ACKNOWLEDGEMENTS

In writing this publication and preparing the exhibition that it accompanies, I have received generous help from a number of people and organisations, notably from Baillie Gifford, the sponsor, and from all those who lent their paintings and objects to the exhibition and allowed photographs of them to be used as illustrations. I should also like to thank the anonymous donor who made possible the production of the map.

I am particularly grateful to Jan Newton, the exhibition designer; Drs Marieke Tiethoff-Spliethoff; Drs L. J. van der Klooster; Drs Marie Christine van der Sman, Director of the Historical Museum, The Hague; Peter van der Ploeg, Curator, Royal Cabinet of Paintings, Mauritshuis; Miss Margaret Hilton; Drs B. Woelderink, Director of the Dutch Royal House Archives; Dr Annette Frese of the Kürpfälzisches Museum, Heidelberg; Elfriede, Matthias and Rudi Kaspar of Frankfurt; Catharine Macleod of the National Portrait Gallery, London; Drs Willem Jan Hoogsteder; Dr May G. Williamson; Mrs Christine McWilliam; Mrs Fiona Buchanan; Mark Weiss of the Weiss Gallery; Stuart McLaren; Wilfried Rogasch of the Deutsches Historisches Museum, Berlin; Dr Alison Rosie; Sara Stevenson and all the other colleagues who helped with the exhibition and publication.

ROSALIND K. MARSHALL
Scottish National Portrait Gallery

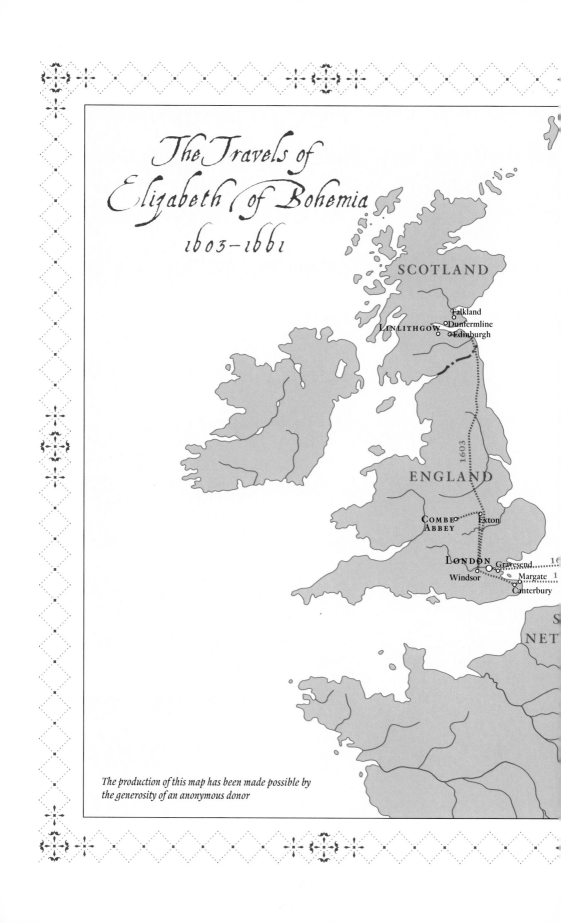

The Travels of
Elizabeth of Bohemia
1603–1661

SCOTLAND

Falkland
Dunfermline
LINLITHGOW Edinburgh

1603

ENGLAND

COMBE Exton
ABBEY

LONDON Gravesend 16
Windsor Margate 1
Canterbury

S
NET

The production of this map has been made possible by
the generosity of an anonymous donor

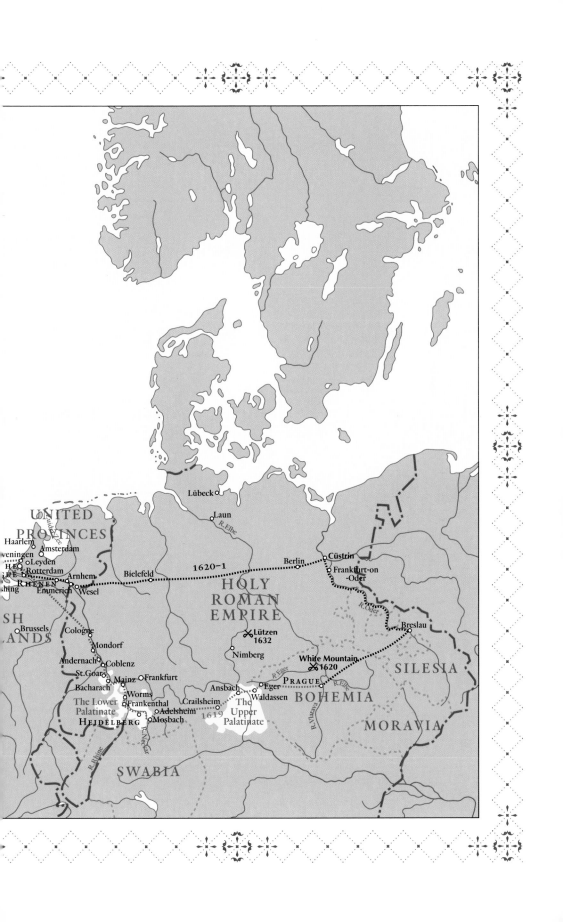

Lübeck

Laun

R.Elbe

UNITED
PROVINCES

Haarlem
veningen
HE
Leyden
Rotterdam
RHENEN
Arnhem
hing
Emmerich
Wesel

Amsterdam

Bielefeld

1620–1

Berlin

Cüstrin

Frankfurt-on
-Oder

HOLY
ROMAN
EMPIRE

R.Oder

Breslau

SH
LANDS

Brussels

Cologne

Mondorf

Andernach
Coblenz
St.Goar
Bacharach
Mainz
Frankfurt
Worms
Frankenthal
The Lower
Palatinate
Adelsheim
HEIDELBERG
Mosbach

R.Rhine

R.Neckar

SWABIA

Lützen
1632

Nimberg

White Mountain
1620

PRAGUE

R.Eger

Ansbach
Eger
Crailsheim
Waldassen
1619
The
Upper
Palatinate

BOHEMIA

R.Vltava

R.Elbe

SILESIA

MORAVIA

CHAPTER ONE
The Child

In a charming portrait of about 1610, by the English artist Robert Peake, a young girl in cream silk sewn with gold stands before a richly decorated chair. Her dress is in the height of fashion, with a fine lace standing collar, a long, pointed bodice and a frounced farthingale skirt. She has a band of jewelled flowers and a huge diamond brooch in her reddish-gold hair, and although she is little more than a child, she wears pearl earrings as well as a pearl necklace. A chain set with diamonds is slung from her right shoulder and a large jewel in the form of a knight on horseback is suspended from the centre of her neckline. The rider may well represent St George, for the design is strongly reminiscent of the badge of the Order of the Garter.

In contrast to all her finery, the sitter's attitude is docile, even submissive. She holds neither flower, fan nor book, those frequent accessories in early seventeenth-century portraits, nor does she rest an arm on a table or on the back of the important chair. Instead, her hands hang limply at her sides and her eyes are slightly downcast. The artist, while emphasising her wealth and status, has also given her an air of meekness and compliance, desirable attributes in an eligible young woman, no matter how wealthy or highborn. Here, at about the age of fourteen, is Princess Elizabeth, eldest daughter of King James VI of Scotland and I of England, as yet unmarried

PLATE 1
Elizabeth of Bohemia, at about the age of fourteen, by Robert Peake
National Portrait Gallery, London

15

PLATE 2
*Falkland Palace, the royal residence
where Elizabeth may have been born, painted by Alexander Kierincx
in the 1630s*
Scottish National Portrait Gallery

and a valuable asset to her father in his diplomatic negotiations, for he could offer her to potential allies as a prospective bride.

Elizabeth had been born in Scotland on 19 August 1596, before her father inherited his English kingdom. Some chroniclers claimed that Falkland Palace, a favourite Stewart hunting lodge, had been her birthplace, while others asserted that her mother, Anne of Denmark, lay in at her own palace of Dunfermline. James certainly held a meeting of his privy council at Dunfermline at the end of September to make arrangements for the baptism but, given the peripatetic nature of the Court, that is not necessarily significant and there remains no conclusive evidence one way or the other.

There is, however, no doubt about the place of the christening. 'Lady Elizabeth, first daughter of Scotland' was baptised on 28 November 1596 in the Chapel Royal at Holyroodhouse, where her grandmother, Mary, Queen of Scots had married her grandfather, Lord Darnley, more than thirty years before. Both were now dead, Darnley after the explosion at Kirk o' Field in 1567, Mary on the scaffold at Fotheringhay in 1587,

PLATE 3	PLATE 4	PLATE 5
Mary, Queen of Scots, Elizabeth's grandmother, by an unknown artist after a miniature of 1578	*Henry Stewart, Lord Darnley, Elizabeth's grandfather, at the age of nine, by Hans Eworth*	*Medal commemorating the marriage of Mary, Queen of Scots and Henry, Lord Darnley in 1565*
Scottish National Portrait Gallery	Scottish National Portrait Gallery	Scottish National Portrait Gallery

executed by the English for plotting against their own Queen, Elizabeth I. James VI had scarcely protested about his mother's death, so anxious was he to avoid jeopardising his chances of succeeding to the English throne. Now, nearly ten years on, he decided to name his new daughter after Elizabeth, inviting her to become the sole godmother. Surely that would persuade her to nominate him as her successor at last.

It did not, of course, have the desired effect, for Elizabeth I fully appreciated the perils of designating an heir who could become a focus for rebellion against her. However, declaring herself to be graciously pleased, she sent Robert Bowes of Aske, Treasurer of Berwick, to represent her at the ceremony. There were no triumphs, outdoor processions or public entertainments in Edinburgh to celebrate the occasion. It was, after all, 'in winter season and ill weather', as one of the royal clerks noted, and a great deal

Prospectus Regis: Palatis LIMNUCHENSIS· *The Prospect of The Royal Palace of* LINLITHGOW.

This plate is Most humbly Inscribed to the Hon.ble Sr James Cunynghame of Milnecraig Bart—

PLATE 6
Linlithgow Palace, where Elizabeth spent her early childhood, engraved by John Slezer in 1693
Scottish National Portrait Gallery

of money had already been spent on the christening of James's son and heir, Prince Henry Frederick, less than two years before. Even so, there was 'good fare and cheer', with large quantities of wild meat and venison served at the baptismal banquet. Violers and taborers played, lackeys had new scarlet cloth liveries, and guests brought presents. Unfortunately, Queen Elizabeth had not sent anything, no doubt feeling that she had done her duty by providing Prince Henry with an unexpectedly large and expensive gold font. There was another disappointment, too, when the ornate casket brought by the Edinburgh bailies was opened. Instead of containing the expected gold coins, it was found to hold a large parchment, promising the new Princess a hundred merks Scots – not now, but when she eventually married.

Soon after the ceremony, the baby was taken to Linlithgow by Lord and Lady Livingston, who were to look after her. Anne of Denmark had strong maternal feelings and her initially harmonious relationship with her husband had already been ruined by a series of violent quarrels about her separation from her first child. Following royal custom, James had decreed that Prince Henry should be given into the keeping of the Earl of Mar at Stirling Castle, where he would be brought up with his own household. Desperately upset, Anne had stormed, raged and pleaded, but all to no purpose. James remained adamant.

Concentrating on her desperate annoyance about her son, Anne made less demur when Elizabeth was installed in Linlithgow Palace with her wet-nurse Bessie MacDowall, her Mistress Nurse, Alison Hay, and her Keeper of Coffers, Elizabeth Hay. At about this time, Prince Henry had his portrait painted, sitting in his high chair, wearing expensive, lace-trimmed garments. No such early picture of Elizabeth survives to show how she looked, but the accounts of the Lord High Treasurer of Scotland record expenditure on her dresses of crimson and yellow satin, figured velvet and Spanish taffeta, her silk stockings, her hairbrush and the four dolls which cost half a merk each. In 1598 she was joined in the royal nurseries by a new sister named Margaret, who died in 1600 at the age of two. That

THREDERICVS · HENRI
VS · D · G · PRINCEPS ·
SCOTORVM · ÆTATIS ·
VÆ · 2 · 1596 ·

PLATE 7
Prince Henry Frederick, Elizabeth's elder brother, at the age of two, by an unknown artist
Private Collection

same year her second brother, the future Charles I was born, a delicate child, and two years after that there was another baby boy, Robert, who survived for only a few months.

On 23 March 1603, James VI achieved his lifelong ambition when Queen Elizabeth I died and he inherited the English throne. A fortnight later he set off for London, taking a public farewell of his wife, in front of tearful Edinburgh crowds. Anne was pregnant again, but she miscarried and it was not until 1 June that she began her journey, joyfully reunited with Prince Henry and Princess Elizabeth, who were to accompany her. Prince Charles would stay in Scotland until he was stronger. Because she was 'not able to undertake great journeys as Her Majesty did', six-year-old Elizabeth travelled shorter distances each day, keeping to the main route while her mother made frequent diversions to visit the leading nobility of each district through which they passed. Sometimes the Princess arrived at major stopping places before the rest of the royal party. At Huntingdon, for example, she was there before them and was given a formal reception, with wine and sweetmeats.

PLATE 8
Silver medal commemorating the accession of King James VI of Scotland to the throne of England in 1603
Scottish National Portrait Gallery

One of the principal pleasures of the long journey to join her father at Windsor seems to have been the opportunity of becoming better acquainted with her brother. They had met before, of course, presumably on trips to Edinburgh for state occasions, but these had been all too brief. Now they had long talks, and they discovered a close affinity. Both had the quick Stewart intelligence, were energetic and fond of riding and the outdoor life. More than that, of course, they shared the bond of being royal children, set apart from even the highest aristocracy, conscious always that their father was the King. In Scotland, Court manners were less formal than they were elsewhere. The powerful nobles never forgot that the Stewart monarchs were descended from an aristocratic family no different from themselves, and many of James's subjects were apt to treat him with scant respect. It was not so long before that one of the ministers of the church had importunately plucked at his sleeve and reminded him that he was merely one of God's weak vassals, like everyone else.

James had rather different ideas about kingship, and he had already set down his convictions about the divine right of kings to rule in a book that he had written for his eldest son. However, it amused him to affect an air of homely intimacy, teasing his councillors, giving them nicknames, address-ing his wife in public as 'my Annie' and referring to his children as 'the bairns'. He might warn Prince Henry not to put on airs when they got to London, with the characteristically pithy observation that 'A king's son and heir was ye before, and no more are ye yet', but of course no one was more delighted than James himself to be moving to a country where the monarch was treated with the deference befitting God's chosen ruler.

PLATE 9
King James VI and I, Elizabeth's father,
painted in 1604 by an unknown artist
Scottish National Portrait Gallery

PLATE 10
Queen Anne of Denmark, Elizabeth's
mother, by Paul van Somer, 1617
Earl of Southesk

The royal cavalcade finally arrived at Windsor on 30 June 1603, to be greeted by huge crowds of people. There had been no young princes and princesses in England since the days of Henry VIII and now, although their new monarch was not particularly personable, his wife and children were tall and handsome. Delighted to show them off, James lifted up Elizabeth and kissed her, smiling at his wife, asking a bystander with obvious pride, 'if he did not think his Annie looked passing well, and my little Bessie too', and adding that his daughter was 'not an ill-favoured wench and may outshine her mother one of these days.'

Elizabeth attended her brother's installation as a Knight of the Garter on 2 July, and made a favourable impression on the French ambassador during the celebrations. Her father was toying with the notion of marrying her to the Dauphin, the son and heir of Henri IV of France, one of whose daughters would at the same time become the bride of Prince Henry. Elizabeth was, the ambassador reported, 'very well bred and handsome enough, rather tall for her age, and her disposition very gentle, rather melancholy than gay.' She was probably overwhelmed with all the excitement and the sight of so many new faces.

After spending a few weeks with Henry at the royal palace of Oatlands, she was taken in October to Exton in Rutlandshire and then on to Combe Abbey in Warwickshire, the home of her new guardians, Lord and Lady

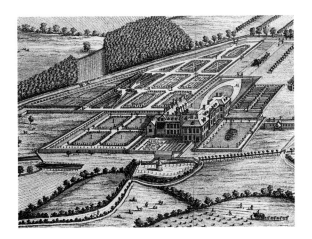

PLATE 12

Elizabeth of Bohemia in 1603 at the age of seven,
soon after her arrival in England, attributed to Robert Peake

National Maritime Museum, Greenwich

Harington. Her portrait, painted in the early autumn of that year, shows her standing in a wooded landscape, her hair elegantly done up with pearls and rubies, jewelled bows decorating her dress, a fan in her left hand and her farthingale skirt fashionably hitched up in front to show the red fringed hem of her underskirt. In the background, riders emerge from the woods and two elegant ladies are seated among the trees.

Combe Abbey was indeed a pleasant setting, a handsome house built round three sides of a quadrangle and surrounded by wooded parkland. The burden of looking after a princess was financially challenging, despite extra allowances from the Exchequer, and there were constant worries about the security, health and education of a royal child. However, Lord Harington, an earnest Protestant gentleman with grown up daughters of his own, was equal to the task. Elizabeth's household included the familiar figure of Alison Hay the Mistress Nurse as well as a new French lady's maid, a physician, footmen and a laundress, chamber women and grooms. There were also masters of writing, dancing, French, Italian and music. Fearing that she was lonely, Lord Harington brought his niece Anne Dudley to be a companion for her, and allowed the Princess to keep a multiplicity of pets on an island in the grounds of his house.

Elizabeth was good-natured, warm-hearted and generous. She made lasting friendships with Anne and her other ladies, lavished affection on her dogs, monkeys and birds, and longed for the company of her own family, particularly her brother. She saw them all too rarely, on visits to London, but she wrote to them regularly. Her letters were careful exercises in courtly composition, correct in every detail. On her father's instructions, she wrote polite little notes to Lady Arabella Stewart, his cousin. She addressed James himself as 'Most gracious sovereign and dear father', signing herself 'Your Majesty's most obedient daughter, Elizabeth'. Henry was 'My dearest brother the Prince.' Deeper feelings were never allowed to disturb this urbane circumlocution, but there was at least one drama in her life. When she was nine, Guy Fawkes and his fellow conspirators planned to blow up the King and Prince in parliament and place her on the throne instead. Lord Harington's prudent precautions kept her safe, but months later he commented that 'this poor lady hath not yet recovered the surprise, and is very ill and troubled', often exclaiming 'What a Queen should I have been by this means! I had rather have been with my royal father in the Parliament House than wear his crown on such occasion.'

As time passed, she went to London more often, and when she was twelve she was given her own apartments at Hampton Court and Whitehall, and began to make regular public appearances. Court poets composed verses praising her beauty in extravagant terms, writers dedicated their books to her, and ambitious courtiers showered her with gifts of jewellery, sweetmeats, fruit, clothing and pet animals and birds. Rather than listening to flowery compliments, however, she preferred to be out riding with Henry, and when asked to write something in an autograph book, she

PLATE 13
*Lady Arabella Stewart, Elizabeth's childhood correspondent,
painted in 1605, probably by Robert Peake*
Scottish National Portrait Gallery

PLATE 14
Henry Frederick, Prince of Wales, in Garter Robes, attributed to Robert Peake
Earl of Mar and Kellie, on loan to the Scottish National Portrait Gallery

carefully inscribed, in Italian, 'Honesty united to cheerfulness contents me.' No doubt this was a stock phrase for such an occasion, but it summed up accurately enough her happy, uncomplicated nature.

Lord Harington encouraged her friendship with her brother, telling Mr Newton, the Prince's tutor, that he wished with all his heart that the two young people could meet every day, 'to increase the comfort they receive in each other's company'. Prince Charles had come down from Scotland by now, but he was still a delicate child and too young to join in their vigorous activities. James was busy ruling both his kingdoms and, after the early turmoil of her marriage, Anne of Denmark had retreated into an aloof toleration of her husband's more tiresome characteristics. They led friendly enough but largely separate lives. Although she was devoted to her children, especially her sons, people complained that the Queen seemed to prefer paintings to people. She did indeed have a keen, artistic eye, and a great enthusiasm for the elaborate, expensive court masques which combined music, poetry, dance, philosophy and spectacle. As soon as they were old enough, the children were encouraged to participate, Elizabeth appearing in the guise of a nymph in attendance on her mother.

Henry was now growing to manhood and undertaking a variety of duties as Prince of Wales. Athletic, well-educated, interested in shipbuilding, paintings, and international affairs, upright and more than a little priggish, he had become so popular that his father was becoming suspicious of his intentions, while for her part Elizabeth complained that she was not seeing enough of him. They remained devoted to each other, however, and in 1608 the French ambassador was reporting that Henry had promised Elizabeth that he would not marry one of Henri IV's daughters unless she went to France too, as the Dauphin's bride. The ambassador commented that the Princess was 'full of virtue and merit', and it was in this context that the meek portrait of her in the cream and gold dress was painted.

PLATE 15

Elizabeth's bridegroom, Frederick V, Elector Palatine in 1612–13,
a pen and ink drawing on vellum by Sir Balthasar Gerbier,
a Flemish artist at the British Court

British Museum, London

CHAPTER TWO

The Bride

In the end, Elizabeth did not go to France. Her father, who saw himself as the peacemaker of Europe, decided that if he was going to marry his son to a Roman Catholic, his daughter must have a Protestant husband. So it was that on Sunday, 18 October 1612 a small, thin young man with dark hair and sensitive features arrived by water at Whitehall to claim Elizabeth as his bride. The ambitious relatives of Frederick, Elector Palatine had seen their opportunity, and after months of negotiation the match had been arranged. Frederick was, according to his friends, suitable in every way. The same age as the Princess, he had a perfect body, they said, an agreeable countenance and he was fluent in French and Latin. His retinue of a hundred and fifty had been equipped with smart new liveries in Palatine blue and the Duke of Würtemberg's dancing master had just spent a month teaching him the latest steps.

The entire royal family turned out to greet him. Prince Charles, twelve years old now, was waiting on the landing stage to escort him into the Banqueting House, where the King was seated on his chair of state, with the Queen, Henry and Elizabeth grouped around him. While the Princess waited with eyes modestly downcast, James rose and embraced him. Overcome by the grandeur and significance of the occasion, Frederick mumbled his speech of thanks, in French, in such a low voice that no one could hear, whereupon James broke in with, 'Say no more about it. Suffice it that I am anxious to testify to you by deeds that you are welcome'.

Gratefully, Frederick moved on to stand before the Queen, who stared at him 'with a fixed countenance'. As the daughter, sister and wife of kings, she was furious that her only daughter was being married to a mere German prince. His grandfather might have been the famous Protestant hero William the Silent, but that did not make up for his lack of status. Ever since the marriage contract had been signed she had been tormenting Elizabeth by addressing her as 'Goodie Palsgrave' as though she were a tradesman's wife. Frederick kissed her hand and she deigned to exchange a few words with him, but her manner remained chilly. Finally, he drew level with Elizabeth and, following the continental custom, made to bend down to kiss the hem of her skirt. She quickly prevented him from doing so by dropping him an unusually low curtsey and then, looking at him shyly at last, she offered him her cheek to kiss. Their eyes met, and they were instantly attracted to each other.

Apart from the Queen, everyone liked him. James presented him with an expensive ring, Henry treated him like a brother, he was given lodgings in all the principal royal palaces, and he was encouraged to spend as much time as possible in Elizabeth's company. Just when everything seemed to be going better than anyone could have expected, Prince Henry fell dangerously ill. He had not been himself for some weeks, suffering from headaches and giddiness. Now, he took to his bed, the royal doctors were summoned, and all visitors were forbidden for fear of infection. Elizabeth was distraught. She knew that he was asking for her repeatedly, and she even tried to get into his chamber in disguise, but it was no use. His temperature continued to rise, and he became delirious. He died on 6 November 1612, probably of typhoid. His last coherent words had been, 'Where is my dear sister?'

In her sorrow, Elizabeth turned to Frederick for consolation, and her love for him deepened as she found in him a sympathetic and understand-

PLATE 16
Charles I, Elizabeth's younger brother, by or after Robert Peake
Scottish National Portrait Gallery

PLATE 17
Frederick V, Elector Palatine,
Elizabeth's future husband, engraved by
Boethius A. Boiswert after Michael
van Mierevelt
Scottish National Portrait Gallery

PLATE 18
King James VI, at the age of twenty-nine,
by Adrian Vanson
Scottish National Portrait Gallery

PLATE 19
Anne of Denmark, at the age of nineteen,
painted by Adrian Vanson the year before
Elizabeth was born
Scottish National Portrait Gallery

OPPOSITE
PLATE 20
Medal struck to mark the wedding of
Elizabeth and Frederick V, Elector Palatine in
1613, with its original die
Yorkshire Museum

ing friend. His father had died some years before, and he knew about grief. The King was devastated by the loss of his heir, but when he had recovered a little he began to wonder if he should not after all provide his daughter with a more high-born bridegroom than the Elector Palatine. If anything happened to Prince Charles, Elizabeth would one day inherit the throne. Frederick's advisers and presumably the young couple themselves were thrown into a panic and pressed for the marriage to go ahead as soon as possible. In the end, the King relented, and on 27 December Elizabeth and Frederick were formally betrothed, she in black satin with a plume of white feathers on her head, he in purple velvet. Anne of Denmark announced that she had gout, and stayed at home.

The wedding took place in the chapel royal at Whitehall on 14 February 1613, St Valentine's Day. This time, Elizabeth was wearing an elaborate dress of cloth of silver, 'upon her head a crown of refined gold, made imperial by the pearls and diamonds thereupon placed, which were so thick beset that they stood like shining pinnacles upon her amber-coloured

hair', as one romantically minded observer put it. Her train was so long that it took fourteen or fifteen ladies dressed in white satin to carry it. Frederick's cloth of silver suit matched Elizabeth's dress and Anne of Denmark, who had been persuaded that even she could not miss her own daughter's marriage, was handsome in white. The King, in sumptuous black, with a particularly expensive diamond in his hat, lost no time in telling everyone that, according to his calculation, the jewellery being worn by Anne, Charles and himself that day was worth nine hundred thousand pounds sterling.

The chapel royal had been hung with cloth of gold, and the young couple stood on a platform strewn with oriental carpets. Elizabeth, it was noticed, was so happy and excited that she seemed on the verge of laughing as the Archbishop of Canterbury pronounced them man and wife. The husband her father had chosen for her had become the man of her choice. Members of the Middle Temple and Lincoln's Inn produced a masque appropriately entitled *The Marriage of Thames and Rhine* and John Donne composed an epithalamium or wedding song, describing the momentous day from dawn, when the 'fair Phoenix Bride' rose to meet 'her Frederick' until night, when 'He comes, and passes through Sphere after Sphere / First her sheets, then her Arms, then any where'. The ensuing days were given up to celebration.

Events in royal circles were always conducted with slow ceremony, and so it was not until two months after the wedding that the newly married couple set off for Germany. The King and Queen accompanied them as far as Rochester, and then they made their way to Canterbury. After a series of delays because of contrary winds, they finally sailed from Margate on board *The Prince Royal*, accompanied by six men-of-war, seven merchant ships and a variety of smaller vessels. The scene was recorded in considerable detail in a painting by Adam Willaerts.

After an uneventful crossing they arrived at Flushing, where Frederick's uncle, the famous soldier Prince Maurice of Nassau, was waiting to welcome them and escort them to The Hague. There was much rejoicing, with banquets, pageants, long speeches and many compliments. Installed in handsome apartments in the Binnenhof, they were showered with expensive wedding presents – diamonds, gold plate, cash and a silver-plated cradle valued at 50,000 guilders. Frederick, looking anxious, had his portrait painted by Michael van Mierevelt, and Elizabeth was taken on a tour of the principal towns of the Low Countries. She then sailed up the Rhine while he rode ahead to make sure that everything in his castle at Heidelberg was in perfect order for her arrival.

Seated on deck under a canopy supported by imitation marble pillars, Elizabeth spent her days gliding along the river, watching more pageants and more celebrations, her nights in castles on the west bank. At first it was interesting, but the novelty soon palled and when Frederick appeared

PLATE 21

The Embarkation of the Elector Palatine and Princess Elizabeth at Margate in 1613,
on their way to Heidelberg, by Abraham Willaerts
Lent by Her Majesty The Queen

unexpectedly one day she persuaded him to let her make the rest of the journey by coach. She finally entered Heidelberg on 7 June 1613, wearing a cloth of gold dress and a scarlet, high-crowned hat. Tall and well made like her grandmother, Mary, Queen of Scots, she was noticeably larger than her small, slight husband, but her imposing size was seen as an advantage. She would be able to bear many sons.

Her new subjects were impressed, and so must she have been. Frederick's handsome red sandstone castle, now largely ruined, is set high above the old university town of Heidelberg, looking out over the wide, flat valley of the River Neckar. At one end of the castle is the original Gothic round tower, flanked by two splendid Renaissance buildings linked by a Hall of Mirrors. The façade of the Ottoheinrichsbau is decorated with statues of the Virtues, Old Testament heroes and classical gods and goddesses, while the adjoining Friedrichsbau, erected by Frederick's father in 1607, has sixteen large statues of his ancestors in niches. 'The English building', a somewhat austere structure whose main external feature is a double row of large, plain windows, had been erected by Frederick himself in contemplation of his marriage. Across the courtyard, the early sixteenth-century Library contained not only the privately owned books

PLATE 22
Frederick V Elector Palatine,
painted by Michael van Mierevelt in The
Hague in 1613, on his way to Heidelberg
Royal Cabinet of Paintings, Mauritshuis,
The Hague

PLATE 23
Engraving of Frederick welcoming
Elizabeth to Heidelberg, from Beschreibung
der Reiss, a volume of engravings of her
journey to Germany
British Library Board

PLATE 24
Heidelberg Castle,
engraved by U. Kraus
Kürpfälzisches Museum der Stadt
Heidelberg

of the Prince Electors but their collection of paintings, and the electoral Mint.

A huge triumphal arch had been put up in the Great Courtyard, featuring figures not only of previous Electors Palatine but of Elizabeth's own ancestors, and a large crowd of relatives, friends, neighbours and their retinues had gathered, eager to see their Prince's prestigious bride. She greeted them all with enthusiasm and unaffected charm, and for several days the guests were entertained to banquets and entertainments, Frederick himself playing the part of Jason in one of the celebratory masques.

Elizabeth and Frederick began their life together in sumptuous style. Their private apartments were on the upper floors of the two Renaissance wings, and when entertaining on the grand scale they held banquets in the Glass Hall. Completed in 1549, it was so called because of the large and expensive Venetian glass windows in its top-floor banqueting chamber. They installed a small theatre near their own rooms, for the performance of masques, and began collecting and commissioning fine tapestries. They also turned their attention to the castle grounds. There was already a wide terrace with a panoramic view of the Neckar, but Frederick and Elizabeth decided to create a formal garden in the Italian style.

Salomon de Caus, a gifted landscape gardener, had already worked for Elizabeth's father and her brother Henry at Greenwich and Richmond. Summoned to Heidelberg, he devised an elaborate scheme and, under his direction, hundreds of workmen blasted rock, levelled mounds, built supporting walls, constructed terraces and dug out numerous flights of steps. Pipes were laid, fountains installed and statues set up. Before long there was an orangery, fruit grew in greenhouses, fish swam in special pools, music played and water tumbled over rocks in a shell-encrusted grotto. On the fourth of his five terraces, Frederick erected life-size statues of Elizabeth and himself. This was not his only romantic gesture. According to legend, the handsome triumphal arch of sandstone leading into the former Gun Garden was built in one night as a surprise present for her.

PLATE 25
Frederick and Elizabeth's famous garden at Heidelberg Castle,
from 'Hortus Palatinus', the book published by its designer, Salomon de Caus, in 1620
British Library Board

Elizabeth had soon settled down to a new way of life which was largely familiar to her. 'Madame', wrote one of the courtiers at Heidelberg not long after her arrival, 'takes her pleasure in hunting and is become a second Diana of our shady Rhine-side woods'. Despite persistent reports that she was pregnant, she continued her energetic riding throughout the autumn, ignoring even the remonstrations of her father, who had heard the rumours. When questioned, she blankly denied that she was expecting a child. The thought that she might really be pregnant never seems to have entered her head. On 2 January 1614, however, she gave birth to a large and healthy son, and was forced to write to her relatives explaining that her previous denials had been caused by her 'naive disposition'. Although she had not contemplated motherhood so soon, she was delighted with her

39

'black baby', for he bore a strong resemblance to her husband. They named him Frederick Henry, after his father and his dead uncle, amidst much rejoicing, not only in the Palatinate but in Britain. This was James VI and I's grandson, after all, and his birth made more secure the Protestant succession. In Edinburgh, bonfires were lit and a salute was fired from the Castle guns.

Sir Dudley Carleton, James's Ambassador at Venice, visited Heidelberg in the autumn of 1615 and sent back a glowing report. 'Their Highnesses, God be thanked, are very well and love one another more than ever. Madame is, at this moment, playing with and caressing her little Prince.' Sir Henry Wotton, his rival and successor, was equally enthusiastic. 'My Lady your gracious daughter,' he wrote, 'retaineth still her former virginal verdure in her complexion and features, though she be now the mother of one of the sweetest children that I think the world can yield.' He added, however, that in his view Frederick had not grown much since his wedding, either in height or breadth. 'He is merry, but for the most part cogitate (or as they call it here, melancholique)'. Elizabeth had realised early on in their

ELISABETHA BOHEMIÆ REGINA MAGNÆ BRITANNIÆ PRINCEPS PALATINA RHENI ELECTRIX &c:

LEFT TO RIGHT:

PLATE 26

Elizabeth on horseback, 1612–13, by an unknown engraver
British Museum, London

PLATE 27

Sir Dudley Carleton, Viscount Dorchester, who visited Heidelberg in 1615 and became a close friend of Elizabeth and Frederick, by Michael van Mierevelt
National Portrait Gallery, London

PLATE 28

Sir Henry Wotton, the diplomat and poet who wrote the famous lines, 'You meaner beauties of the night' in Elizabeth's honour, painted by an unknown artist
National Portrait Gallery, London

relationship that her husband was subject to bouts of black depression, and at those times even she found it difficult to divert him.

He had reason enough to be gloomy, of course, for the continuing post-Reformation struggle between Roman Catholics and Protestants dominated the European scene, and was already affecting their personal life. Frederick did not spend all his time laying out gardens, hunting with Elizabeth and planning delightful surprises. As First Elector of the Holy Roman Empire he occupied an influential position, and as a convinced Calvinist he was the leading member of the Union of Protestant Princes, which his father had founded to meet the threat from the Roman Catholic Holy Roman Emperor. Since the Calvinist and Lutheran members of the Union were constantly quarrelling with each other, Frederick spent a great deal of time engaged in delicate negotiations in different parts of Germany.

When he was away, Elizabeth had to wrestle with the problems of running her household. Young and inexperienced as she was, she did not find it easy, and members of her retinue were all too ready to take advantage of her good nature. Frederick's High Steward, Count Meinhard von

Schonberg, did his best to offer advice. Always known to the British as Colonel Schonberg, he was the rejected suitor of Anne Dudley, Elizabeth's childhood friend, who had come to Heidelberg as her chief lady. Perhaps he might gain her favour if he helped.

'Never grant anything on the first request, but answer to all, "I will consider – I will think of it – I will see"', he urged Elizabeth. 'Never be teased into countermanding an order ... Prevent gossiping between servants of all grades ... Never allow reports of one about another, nor importunate solicitations, nor care when they take offence. Be generally more severe.' Elizabeth tried, but it was not in her nature to be strict. Softhearted and always ready to be a sympathetic listener, she never could resist a plea for help, and as she was frequently asked for money, her finances were chaotic. She was nonetheless grateful for the Colonel's advice, and with her encouragement, Anne accepted his proposal, only to die after childbirth within a year. A few months later, he himself was dead.

He had offered words of advice for Frederick, too, reminding him that public appearances were part of his role in life and telling him that he must pretend to be enjoying them even if he were not in the mood. Above all, he must not look morose and preoccupied, for such behaviour would drive people away. These comments probably made Frederick feel more depressed than ever but Elizabeth, full of loving concern, knew that the best remedy for his depression was an interlude in the country away from all his troubles. A six-week trip to the Upper Palatinate in the summer of 1615 improved his health considerably and she was able to tell friends, 'I hope his melancholy is so past as it will not return in that height'.

Her little boy was eighteen months old now, and as time went by she began to worry that she had not become pregnant again. However, on 22 December 1617 she gave birth to her second son. A premature baby, he was very small at birth, but he soon picked up and within a fortnight he was thriving well. They named him Charles Louis, after Elizabeth's brother and Frederick's. In 1618 their first daughter, Elizabeth, was born. A few weeks afterwards upsetting news came from England. Anne of Denmark had died. Elizabeth wrote at once to her father, telling him that words could not express how deeply she felt this loss, which she would regret all her life. Her distress was all the keener because she had hoped to visit London the previous year, but had been forced to cancel her plans because of her pregnancy. James was in poor health too, but there was no prospect of a journey to England in the immediate future because the long-standing religious disputes in the Holy Roman Empire had erupted into a new crisis involving Frederick himself.

PLATE 29

Elizabeth and her infant son, Prince Frederick Henry, about 1615, drawn by Nicholas Hilliard

British Museum, London

PLATE 30

The Election of Frederick V as King of Bohemia, by an unknown engraver

British Museum, London

CHAPTER THREE

The Queen

The kingdom of Bohemia was part of the Holy Roman Empire, but many of its subjects were Protestant. Hitherto, its monarchs had been elected. The ageing Holy Roman Emperor Matthias now held the title himself but, anxious to make Bohemia's throne hereditary, he managed to pass it to his cousin and adopted heir, Ferdinand of Styria. Ferdinand was an enthusiastic Roman Catholic, and soon the alarmed Protestants of Bohemia were complaining to the Emperor that their new king was treating them with unjustifiable severity. Matthias ignored their pleas and upheld Ferdinand's authority. Furious, they threw two of Ferdinand's leading councillors from the windows of the council chamber, in a famous incident known as the Defenestration of Prague. Surprisingly, the councillors survived, but the incident was the signal for Protestant rebellion.

Frederick, Elector Palatine was one of the mediators appointed to remedy the situation and he anxiously sought his father-in-law's advice. Still determinedly pursuing his policy of preserving the balance of power in the interests of peace, James VI and I replied that he had no money for war. He did, however, renew his alliance with the Protestant Princes of the Union. In March 1619, before the matter could be resolved, Matthias died, and Ferdinand of Styria was elected Emperor. The Council of Bohemia promptly deposed him as their King, declaring that he had violated his coronation oaths. In his place they unanimously elected Frederick, amidst great rejoicing. They then wrote to him, announcing that he had been chosen, and sent a letter to Elizabeth too, begging her to persuade her husband to accept and to ask her father for assistance.

Frederick was greatly perturbed when he heard the news. He was away from home and he wrote at once to his wife, asking her what he should do. Elizabeth replied that, since God directs all, he had doubtless sent this. She added that she would leave the decision to Frederick, but if he did decide to accept, she would do everything she could to support him. He and she then wrote to all their relatives and friends, asking for their opinion. Frederick's mother, Louisa Juliana, begged him not to endanger the Palatinate, his own inheritance, for the sake of helping a foreign country. Weeks passed without any reply from James VI and I, but there were rumours that he regarded the enterprise as a rash, dangerous and expensive adventure which would destroy any chance of peace in Europe. The Archbishop of Canterbury wrote to say that the defence of the Bohemian Protestants was a noble duty which could not be ignored. Fourteen of Frederick's council of eighteen advisers were against his accepting the crown, but his friend Prince Christian of Anhalt and his chaplain urged him on.

Still he hesitated, tortured by vivid imaginings of the disasters which might lie ahead. He knew very well that a Protestant King of Bohemia, surrounded by his Roman Catholic enemies, would have a hard struggle to survive, and he dreaded the effect on his family. At the same time, he felt that he had to do his best for the Bohemians. His only aim, he said, was 'to employ all that I have in this world for the service of Him who has given it to me.' Like his father-in-law, he believed that kings were chosen by God and must fulfil their responsibilities, come what might. He returned to Heidelberg and Elizabeth listened hour after hour to his earnest, even tearful requests for her advice.

Subsequently, their enemies accused her of forcing her reluctant husband to accept the crown in order to gratify her own ambition. That is a hostile interpretation of events. With her mild, affectionate nature she allowed the men in her life to take the lead: her father the King, of course; Lord Harington, her governor; her brother Henry and now her husband.

As she had told Frederick at the start of the crisis, she was ready to go along with whatever decision he made, but he simply could not decide what to do. Seeing him sink ever deeper into gloom she tried to rally him, joking that he should not have married a King's daughter if he had not the courage to become a King himself. They might lose all their possessions, he replied, remembering his mother's warnings. Trying again to make him laugh, Elizabeth remarked that she would rather eat sauerkraut at a King's table than feast on luxuries in an Elector's house and then, when she saw his expression, added gravely that she would part with all her jewels to maintain such a righteous and religious cause.

Even then he could not make up his mind, and sought the advice of the Protestant Union. The Princes unanimously urged him to accept, as did the States-General of Holland, and his respected uncle, Prince Maurice of Nassau. Still waiting anxiously to see how his father-in-law would react, he ordered prayers for divine guidance to be said in all his churches. When envoys from Bohemia arrived to receive his answer, he explained that he could not give it until he had heard from James. They told him bluntly that if he could not commit himself at once, they would elect someone else. At that, Frederick finally agreed to accept the crown.

The decision taken, he immediately fell into a panic about Elizabeth. Perhaps he should send her back to England while he went to Prague, or maybe she should stay at Heidelberg. She herself had no doubts. Of course she would go with him. Nothing would persuade her to be parted from him. Deeply pessimistic about the entire enterprise, his mother arrived to take charge at the Castle, and it was decided that the two younger children should stay behind with her. Charles Louis and Elizabeth were far too small to undertake the long journey but Frederick Henry, the heir, would go with his parents. Even as they were making their final preparations, James VI and I gave his verdict on the enterprise. The Elector Palatine had rashly entered into the affair without his consent. He was young, so there might be some excuse for him, James observed, but he himself was an old and experienced king and he would do nothing until he was assured that

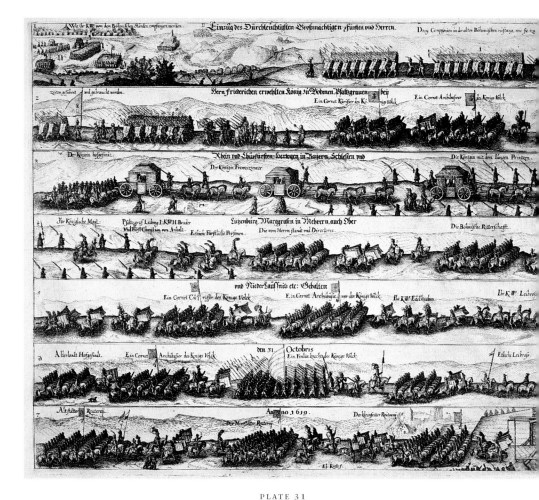

PLATE 31
The Procession of Frederick and Elizabeth entering Prague, by an unknown engraver
British Museum, London

his son-in-law's election was lawful. Only then would he make a decision
as to whether he would help, and he would certainly not embroil his subjects in an unjust war.

News of his reaction did not arrive in Germany until the new King and
Queen of Bohemia were on their way to Prague. They left Heidelberg on
7 October 1619, Frederick on horseback, Elizabeth in a coach, because she
was seven months pregnant. With them went 800 horsemen and many of

48

their household. There were entire families of retainers, like John Albert, Count of Solms and Braunfels, Frederick's Lord Chamberlain and his three motherless daughters. Ursula, the eldest, was married to Count Dohna, another of the chamberlains. Amalia, the middle sister, was one of Elizabeth's favourite ladies, and Louise, the youngest, still only fourteen, was also a member of her household. A hundred and fifty-three wagons were needed for all the luggage, which ranged from gold plate to Jacko, the monkey sent to Elizabeth from Venice by her friend Sir Dudley Carleton.

She was in tears as she went to her coach, but once they were on their way her customary good spirits returned and even a nasty accident could not quench the general excitement. As they approached Ansbach, the wheels of her coach struck a large stone, which shot up and hit her on the leg. The pain was so intense that she fainted, but after a halt at a nearby inn, she insisted on continuing, lying sideways along the seat of the coach. By the time she reached Ansbach, she was herself again.

On 14 October 1619, in Waldassen Castle, the Bohemian envoys solemnly offered Frederick the crown, he accepted and Elizabeth made a gracious speech in French. The next day, they crossed into Bohemia, making their way to the Star Palace, a white-walled, copper-roofed hunting-lodge set in woodlands on the lower slopes of the White Mountain, six miles from Prague. They began the last part of their journey on 31 October, Frederick on horseback in a sumptuous brown and silver suit, Elizabeth seated in a magnificent gold and silver chariot. Huge crowds were waiting to greet them all along the way, and the young couple were reduced to helpless laughter at the incongruous sight of a regiment of four hundred peasants brandishing scythes, flails and hatchets and shouting loudly 'Long live the King', in Latin.

Primitive some of their subjects might seem to be, but as the new King and Queen looked towards their capital, they saw a magnificent sight. St Vitus Cathedral dominates the skyline, with the towers and spires of palaces, churches, chapels and monasteries clustered around it. Prague Castle is a complex of buildings, grouped about two large, linked courtyards,

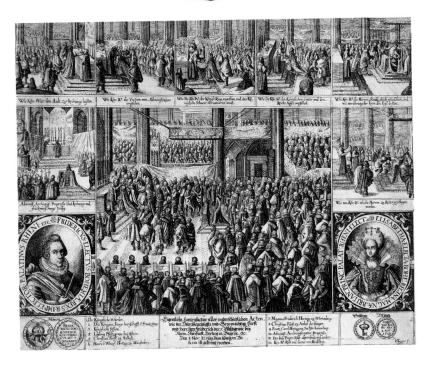

PLATE 32
The Coronation of Frederick V as
King of Bohemia, engraved by E. Kieser
after an unknown artist
Scottish National Portrait Gallery

PLATE 33
Medal commemorating the coronations
of Frederick and Elizabeth as King and
Queen of Bohemia, 1619
British Museum, London

with the royal residence opposite the Cathedral. Elizabeth was to lodge in
the newest part, which had been built by the Emperor Rudolph II, while
Frederick occupied the fourteenth-century wing. She did not want to be
separated from him, however, and so they both stayed in his gloomy,
medieval apartments.

Next morning, they walked to the Great Gallery, to inspect the magnificent collection of Old Master paintings, sculpture, medals, coins, clocks and all manner of other costly curiosities which had been assembled by Rudolph II. Observers noted that Elizabeth took a keen interest in everything. Both her mother and her brother, Prince Henry, had been passionate collectors, and she was well informed and enthusiastic. Laughing delightedly at the sight of so many treasures, she remarked, 'Really, Ferdinand has left us many beautiful things!' 'These things are no longer his, Madame', one of her gentlemen reminded her portentously.

So relieved were the Bohemian Protestants to be replacing Roman Catholic Ferdinand with Calvinist Frederick that they were determined to crown him as soon as possible. There were difficulties, of course. The coronation would take place in St Vitus Cathedral with all its elaborate statues and reliquaries. Frederick ordered the removal of the cross and all the gilded statues which usually stood on the high altar, and decreed that the service would be conducted by Protestant clergy, but there remained the question of the anointing, a central part of the ceremony which he found abhorrent. He well knew, however, that his enemies would swiftly question the legality of his kingship if he were not anointed in the traditional way, and so in the end he agreed that it should be done. The arrangements were swiftly completed and, that same week, on 4 November 1619, the coronation took place, Elizabeth watching from a specially constructed gallery.

Three days after that, she herself was crowned Queen of Bohemia. She walked in procession to the great Gothic cathedral, across rich carpets laid on the cobbles of the square, and put on her coronation robes in the ornate Chapel of St Václav, the walls of which were encrusted with semi-precious stones. The organ thundered out and the choir sang as she moved to the High Altar, where Frederick joined her. 'O Reverend Father', he said to the Administrator of the Bishopric of Prague, 'we request that thou wilt deign to bless this our consort, joined to us by God, and decorate her with the Crown Royal to the praise and glory of our Saviour, Jesus Christ'. Elizabeth was then led to a throne draped with cloth of gold. A lesson was read, prayers were said and then she, too, was anointed. The crown of St Elizabeth was placed on her head, and the orb and sceptre were put in her hands.

As she emerged from the cathedral once more, bells rang, cannon fired a salute, Bohemians in national dress sang and danced, and coronation medals were scattered amongst the crowds. Still wearing her crown, she presided over a lavish banquet in the Hall of Homage, served by the wives of leading courtiers. There was no official guest from Britain that day, either in the cathedral or at the banquet, for James VI and I had forbidden his subjects to recognise Frederick and Elizabeth as King and Queen of Bohemia. He could see all too well the trouble that lay ahead, even if they could not.

Meanwhile, Frederick and Elizabeth tried to accustom themselves to their castle, and to the strange language and the stranger customs of their subjects. At first, all the Bohemian courtiers spoke Czech out of a feeling of national pride, but before long it became evident that they were also fluent in German. That made matters much easier but even so, cultural differences gave rise to many day to day complications. Delegations of Bohemians arriving for audiences gazed in ill-concealed surprise at Elizabeth's fashionable farthingale skirts and her low necklines, while she for her part marvelled at the unusual styles worn by the ladies of the Court. 'This is a very good country', she told the Countess of Bedford in one of her many letters home, 'but the ladies go the strangeliest dressed that ever I saw. They wear all furred capes and furred clothes, and great Spanish ruffs. Their gowns are almost like Spanish fashion, but no farthingales.'

Much more serious were the religious differences. There was still a large community of Roman Catholics in Prague, and they were deeply offended when Frederick's chaplain busied himself arranging the removal of statues

PLATE 34

Elizabeth of Bohemia by Gerard van Honthorst,
painted in exile in 1634 but showing her with the symbols of monarchy
Kürpfälzisches Museum der Stadt Heidelberg

from all the churches. Again, when some of the citizens' wives were granted an audience with Elizabeth a few days after her coronation, they presented her with small, flower-shaped loaves commemorating her name-sake, St Elizabeth of Hungary. They were mortified when she gazed at these uncomprehendingly, and then allowed her pages to stick them in their caps, apparently oblivious of their religious significance.

Tales of the women's annoyance were repeated to her, of course, and after that she tried hard to avoid offending local sensibilities. When another delegation arrived at the castle with an ebony and ivory cradle studded with precious stones, and a matching casket containing a complete set of lace-trimmed baby clothes, she thanked the citizens' wives with a carefully learned sentence in Czech but then embarrassed them by shaking them vigorously by the hand, in the British fashion. Nonetheless, her popularity soared when she gave birth to a fine, healthy prince on 7 December 1619, and the very next day had him put on show in her ante-chamber, in the expensive new cradle.

The baby's christening was delayed, partly because it would be better to wait until spring to allow guests to travel to Prague more easily, and partly because Frederick was fully occupied. He had already been back to the Palatinate to try to reconcile the quarrelling Calvinists and Lutherans, and then as soon as the Christmas festivities were over, he set off for Moravia to accept the homage of his subjects there. Left behind in the vast castle, Elizabeth felt lonely and depressed, not least because she knew that people were saying that their stay in Prague would be of short duration. Indeed, the Jesuits were openly referring to Frederick as 'The Winter King', who would vanish with the snows in spring. As usual, she consoled herself by writing numerous letters, telling her father cheerfully that she and the children were in very good health, but pouring out her unhappiness at such length to her husband that he wrote back with a touch of impatience, 'Certes, you have no reason to think that I have forgotten you or that you are a moment out of my thoughts'.

He was back again by the end of March, in time for his new son's christening, and for a few hours they were able to forget their troubles. The baby was to be called after his ancestor, Rupert III, who had been elected both Emperor and King of Bohemia in 1400. Frederick's ally Bethlen Gabor, the Prince of Transylvania, had agreed to be godfather. Although he did not attend in person, Count Turzo, his proxy, was there in Hungarian national costume with a steel helmet on his head and representatives from Moravia and Silesia attended in full armour. After the service was over all the important ladies in the cathedral were allowed to hold the baby in their arms for a few minutes. The congregation then went outside to admire Bethlen Gabor's gift for the new Prince, a Turkish stallion with jewelled saddle and harness. The subsequent baptismal feast lasted for seven hours. Less than a fortnight later, there was another lavish ceremony when Rupert's eldest brother, Prince Frederick Henry, was proclaimed Crown Prince of Bohemia.

PLATE 35
The Triumph of the Reformation, showing Frederick,
Elizabeth and the Protestants victorious over Roman Catholics, by an unknown engraver
Scottish National Portrait Gallery

CHAPTER FOUR

The Fugitive

Outward show was all very well, but the political situation was growing worse by the day. Furious at everything that had happened in Bohemia, the Emperor Ferdinand ordered Frederick to resign his crown within a month. Frederick replied imprudently that it was for him, as Elector Palatine, to judge the Emperor, it was not for the Emperor to judge him. He then took Elizabeth hunting and throughout that strange summer seemed surprisingly unperturbed by the threatening situation around him. Meanwhile, sitting in Greenwich Park, Elizabeth's friend Sir Henry Wotton wrote his celebrated poem in honour of the Winter Queen:

> *You meaner beauties of the night,*
> *That poorly satisfy our eyes*
> *More by your number than your light,*
> *You common people of the skies;*
> *What are you when the moon shall rise?*

Back in Prague once more, Frederick and Elizabeth tried their best to placate their increasingly critical subjects. On the very hot days, men and women bathed together in the River Vltava. Frederick, always a keen swimmer, had swum in the Thames when he was in London, and he now joined in while Elizabeth watched from a shady position on the bank. Instead of being gratified by this gracious gesture, the Bohemians were horrified. A King should be dignified at all times, they told each other, and no lady would have watched men bathing as Elizabeth had done. Worse followed when Frederick's chaplain had a large and particularly revered bronze crucifix secretly removed from the bridge over the Vltava under cover of darkness. When the citizens discovered next morning that it was missing, they marched angrily on the castle and demanded its return. Frederick had to give way.

Trying to improve matters, Elizabeth decided that she would be served by Bohemians at the next public feast instead of by officials of her own household. This proved disastrous, for the cupbearer spilt wine over her skirt, the server let the meat slide from the plate as he gave it to her, and the gentleman bearing her sugar dropped it and fled when one of her pet monkeys jumped up and tried to steal a lump from the dish he was carrying. Nothing seemed to be going right.

In August 1620, Sir Francis Nethersole arrived in Prague to be Elizabeth's English secretary, and less than a fortnight later he was reporting back to London on 'the dangerous, almost desperate, state of affairs of this kingdom'. The Roman Catholic League had not just one army but four, and they were closing in on Frederick's territories. Half his courtiers did not seem to appreciate the danger, while the other, more experienced men took a defeatist attitude and said that there was no use putting up any defence against the all-powerful Emperor. Ferdinand and Frederick were diametrically opposed and the only possible outcome, in the opinion of Sir Francis, was 'that in the end one of them must, of necessity, be ejected out of the Empire'.

He was right. Within days, Ambrogio Spinola had entered the Palatinate with an army of 25,000 imperial troops and was marching on Heidelberg. Frederick's mother, her worst fears realised, took her grandchildren Charles Louis and Elizabeth and fled. 'My only dear brother', Elizabeth wrote anxiously to Prince Charles on 15 September 1620, 'I am sure you have heard before this, that Spinola hath taken some towns in the Lower Palatinate, which makes me to trouble you with these lines, to beseech you earnestly to move His Majesty [their father] that now he would assist us ... his slackness to assist us doth make the Princes of the Union slack too ... The King hath ever said that he would not suffer the Palatinate to be taken; it was never in hazard but now ...'

Eventually, James sent 2,000 volunteers to help his son-in-law, but in the meantime Maximilian, Duke of Bavaria, head of the Catholic League had already entered Bohemia with another army of 25,000 men and he now joined up with the Imperial Army to march on Prague. As the courtiers from Heidelberg hastily sent their wives and families away to places of safety, Frederick was distraught with worry about Elizabeth and their children. 'The King himself hath this thought both in his heart and head, day and night, and is more troubled therewith than with all the other thorns of his crown', said Sir Francis. After much discussion it was agreed that Frederick's younger brother, Louis, should slip away secretly to Holland early one morning, taking with him young Prince Frederick Henry and several large bags containing Elizabeth's jewels.

She herself refused to seek safety. She was six months pregnant but in vain did they all try to persuade her to go home to England or at least to somewhere in the north of Germany while Frederick marched against the

PLATE 37
Prague Castle and St Vitus Cathedral,
detail from an engraving of the Battle of the White Mountain, 1620
Bayerisches Armeemuseum, Ingolstadt

enemy. Nothing would move her. It would lower morale if she went, she said, and in any case nowhere was safe. Her place was in Prague, and there she would stay. Finally, Frederick had to leave, the problem unresolved. The best he could do was to make sure that she was as safe as possible, guarded by three companies of men, his chief officers of state and his personal bodyguard. 'Spinola is still in the Low Palatinate', Elizabeth wrote to tell one of her father's courtiers on 14 October, 'fortifying those places he hath taken, and the Union looks on, and doth nothing. The King [Frederick] is gone to the Army. It is but seven miles hence, and the enemy's army is but two miles beyond them …'.

Frederick's men were ill equipped and poorly clad, but he said nothing about that in his frequent letters to his wife, as he strove to reassure her with loving messages: 'My dear and only sweetheart, I kiss you lips, your hands, in imagination, a million times …'. In mid October, desperate to see her, he rode back to Prague and urged her once more to leave. If she stayed on much longer and then was forced to go, it would look as though she were fleeing and she would not want that. 'I would not urge you to leave against your will', he told her earnestly. 'I merely give my opinion … you are so bad at making up your mind.' Two ambassadors from England had arrived, to attempt conciliation, and they added their arguments to his, but she was not to be convinced.

Frederick rejoined his men, but on 7 November he was back in Prague Castle once more, telling her the latest news. The Imperial Army, commanded by Count Johann von Tilly, was only eight miles away, but Frederick was confident that he could march his own men between Prague and the enemy. Even as he spoke, his army was starting to move to the slopes of the White Mountain, beside the Star Park. They were full of confidence. 'That night', one of the English volunteers later remembered, 'we slept securely, as free from doubt as we supposed ourselves quit from danger.'

Next morning there was a heavy fog, and it seemed unlikely that there would be any conflict that day. Elizabeth invited the English ambassadors to dine with Frederick and herself and then escort her to the White Mountain to inspect her husband's troops. Throughout the meal they could hear the sound of distant cannon fire, but they had become accustomed to that during the past few days of skirmishing. Declaring that he would go ahead to see that his army was in readiness to receive Elizabeth, Frederick rose from the table, went outside, mounted his horse and rode from the courtyard, only to be confronted by agitated messengers with the news that Tilly had attacked. Crowds of people were rushing out on to the streets of Prague to see what was happening, as hundreds of panic-stricken soldiers surged down from the White Mountain in utter disarray. Many drowned as they tried to swim across the river, and exhausted survivors gasped out accounts of how the leaderless Bohemians had been routed by Tilly and his men.

At once, Frederick turned his horse, rode back to the Castle and, amidst panic and chaos, hustled his wife into her coach while the ambassadors, her ladies and the rest of the household rushed to and fro carrying as many belongings as they could and piled into the other coaches brought hastily round from the stables. Even Jacko the monkey was safely aboard when Christopher, Baron Dohna, making one last hurried circuit of the rooms to ensure that nothing vital had been left behind, discovered Prince Rupert alone in the deserted nursery. Snatching him up, he just managed to throw him into the final coach as the desperate cavalcade clattered its way out of the castle courtyard, down the hill, over the bridge and into the old part of the city.

Frederick, the English ambassadors, the chiefs of his army and his leading courtiers made their way to the house of one of the principal citizens, to hold a council of war. Elizabeth was there too, and although Frederick was consumed with guilt at his absence from the battlefield, she was completely calm and unafraid. After lengthy debate, they were persuaded that there was no use trying to hold the city against the enemy. Prague was almost impossible to defend at any time, and the survivors of the Battle of the White Mountain were demoralised and completely outnumbered.

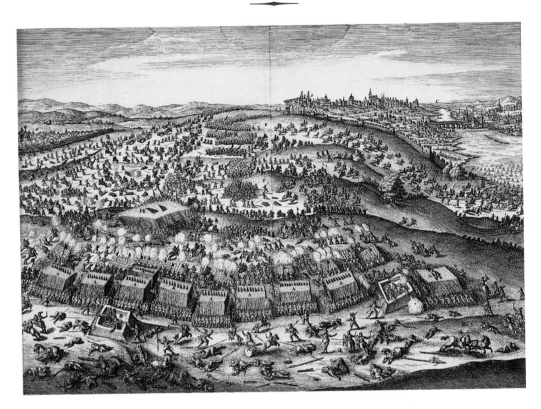

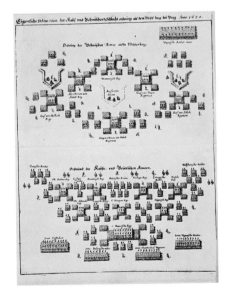

Next morning the royal cavalcade left Prague, Frederick riding alongside the coach containing Elizabeth and Rupert. Behind them followed more than three hundred coaches and wagons.

Convinced that they would be pursued, they hastened eastwards as fast as the appalling condition of the roads in winter would allow. As they reached the border with Silesia, it began to snow, but they dared not stop to wait for conditions to improve. Captain Ralph Hopton took Elizabeth up behind him on his horse and she rode pillion for the next forty miles. When they reached Breslau, Frederick told her that they must part. He was going to turn south into Moravia, where he hoped to rally his men, but she must go northwards, to seek a place of safety for her confinement. He had written to his brother-in-law George William, Elector of Branden-burg, begging him to shelter her. The Elector, terrified of offending the Emperor, delayed and eventually sent a discouraging reply. Spandau was not safe for her and his old castle at Cüstrin was only half-furnished, had no supplies and did not even have a kitchen.

Elizabeth and Frederick spent only one night at Breslau, but Elizabeth found time to pen a desperate plea for help which Baron Dhona would take to her father. The Baron 'will not fail to tell your Majesty of the mis-fortune that has befallen us, and by which we have been compelled to quit Prague', she wrote, and begged him for immediate assistance, 'otherwise I know not what will become of us'. Next morning, she and Frederick said goodbye to each other, unsure that they would ever meet again. Regardless of her brother-in-law's unwelcoming attitude, she had to continue north, and she travelled down the valley of the River Oder, to Frankfurt on Oder. 'I am sure by this time you have had the unwelcome news of our army's

PLATE 38
The Battle of the
White Mountain, 1620,
by an unknown engraver
Bayerisches Armeemuseum,
Ingolstadt

PLATE 39
Johan Ernst,
Duke of Saxe Weimar,
one of the commanders of
Frederick's army, by Michael
van Mierevelt, 1625
Hamilton Collection,
Lennoxlove House

PLATE 40
Plan of the Battle of the
White Mountain, with
Frederick's army on the upper
part of the page, by an
unknown engraver
Bayerisches Armeemuseum,
Ingolstadt

defeat ... ' she wrote from there to Sir Dudley Carleton. 'I am now in the Elector of Brandenburg's country. Tomorrow I go to a fortress of his, where I shall winter. The King sent me hither for fear the enemy should invade Silesia. I am not yet so out of heart, though I confess we are in an evil state, but that (as I hope) God will give us again the victory. For wars are not ended with one battle and I hope we shall have better luck in the next.'

Finally, she arrived at Cüstrin. The Elector of Brandenburg's servants did not dare to refuse her entry, and when she had rested a little she sent him a letter assuring him that she meant to move on to Wolfenbüttel for her confinement. However, the owner of that castle also made excuses, and so she had to stay where she was, anxiously waiting for news of her husband and his army. 'I console myself with one thing. The war is not yet ended', she told her aunt, the Duchesse de la Tremouille. 'I hope that God has only done all this to try us, and doubt not but that for the love of His church He will yet give us the victory ... I stay here this winter in this country, where it seems to me that I am in exile.'

To her surprise and delight, just four days before Christmas, Frederick joined her, but the news he brought was bad. Although the people of Moravia had received him with initial enthusiasm, he had no sooner gone back to Silesia than the Moravian Estates had announced that they were seceding from the Bohemian confederation. The Silesians for their part had made him a gift of eighty thousand florins but, even as they had given it to him, they had begged him to go elsewhere rather than bring down imperial retribution upon them. In tears, he had agreed to move on, telling them in the words of David fleeing from Absalom, 'If I shall find favour in the eyes of the Lord, He will bring me again.'

He was in despair. He realised that he had lost all his allies, and the victorious Imperial leaders had launched a damaging propaganda campaign against him. The Winter King, the King of Hearts (no real king but a mere playing card one), a puny adolescent (although he was twenty-four) who had deserted his own army and run away from the enemy, that was how he was portrayed. Elizabeth was deeply distressed by his humiliation, but she did her best to console and encourage him, and when their fifth child was born on 6 January 1621, she said he must be called after Frederick's uncle, the Prince of Orange, 'Maurice, because he will have to be a fighter.'

On the advice of James VI and I, Frederick wrote to the Holy Roman Emperor offering to resign the crown of Bohemia if he could have the Palatinate back, but it was no use. The request was refused. He then set out for the Hanseatic ports, where he hoped to raise money for a new military campaign. In mid-February, Elizabeth travelled north through heavy snow to Berlin, on her way to join him in Lübeck. She left Maurice with Frederick's sister, the Electress of Brandenburg, who also gave refuge to her own mother Louisa Juliana, along with Charles Louis and little Elizabeth.

When Elizabeth finally met Frederick in Upper Westphalia, it was the middle of March, but at least there was one piece of good news for them. Maurice, Prince of Orange, was offering them refuge. He had even sent an escort to take them to The Hague, where a town house would be placed at their disposal. Elizabeth was greatly relieved, but Frederick was reluctant. He could not wait to retrieve his reputation by leading an expedition to reclaim the Palatinate, and he thought that Elizabeth should retire to the safety of London. Busily trying to marry his son Charles to the daughter of the King of Spain, the Holy Roman Emperor's ally, James VI and I exclaimed, 'God forbid!' when he heard that she might be coming. Much as he loved his daughter, he had no desire to be identified with his son-in-law's disastrous cause.

CHAPTER FIVE

The Exile

The Prince of Orange pressed Frederick and Elizabeth to make up their minds, and when he indicated that he would not keep his offer open forever, they decided to accept his invitation. Travelling by Münster they reached the Rhine, sailed north, and finally arrived in Rotterdam, where they were received with banquets, celebrations and comforting kindness. They then made a triumphal progress to The Hague. Almost the entire population turned out to see them arrive, and Prince Maurice allowed them to stay in the apartments they had occupied during their honeymoon visit until they selected a town house of suitable size. The Hague was already very crowded. There were large numbers of nobles at the Prince's own Court, as well as the visiting diplomats and generals who lodged in the area round the Binnenhof with all their attendants.

Fortunately, two adjacent mansions were available on the Kneuterdijk, just a few moments' walk from the Prince of Orange's residence. Both had belonged to the Grand Pensionary, Johan van Oldenbarnevelt. He himself had lived in the Naaldwijk Hof, while his son-in-law Cornelius van der Myle stayed in the Wassenaer Hof, a rambling red brick mansion set back from the street in its own courtyard. Oldenbarnevelt had been executed three years before, his son-in-law banished and the properties sequestrated, so both houses were available. They were already well furnished, but the States-General of Holland hastily ordered interior alterations and purchased some very grand second-hand furniture for their royal guests.

PLATE 42

Children's Games in The Hague, engraved after Adriaen van der Venne, about 1630.
The Wassenaer Hof is just out of sight on the extreme left, Oldenbarnevelt's is the elaborate mansion beside it, and next door is the Kloosterkerke

Haags Gemeentearchief; photograph by courtesy of the Haags Historisch Museum

PLATE 43

Maurice, Count of Nassau and Prince of Orange, Frederick's uncle, by an unknown artist

Blair Castle Collection, Perthshire

Frederick and Elizabeth took up residence there in April 1621. An inventory made many years later when the furnishings had long since grown shabby nevertheless indicates the splendour in which they lived in the Wassenaer Hof. The oak-panelled outer hall was hung with Flemish tapestries and paintings and had an ornately carved stone fireplace. Their dining room had wall-coverings of fashionable gilded leather. Elizabeth slept in a canopied bed hung with cloth of silver fringed with gold and lined with a pretty flowered fabric, and Jacko the monkey perched beside the writing desk in her cabinet as if he had always been there. The best bedchamber was done in crimson and gold, while other bedchambers were furnished in white, orange and Palatinate blue.

With the royal exiles had come not only their immediate attendants, like the Count of Solms and Braunfels and his daughters, but a host of lesser people so that their entire retinue numbered more than two thousand. The able-bodied men were offered places in the Prince of Orange's army, but many of those who had fled from Prague were women and children, and they had to be found accommodation in the houses nearby and some means of sustenance.

Fortunately, Prince Maurice and the Dutch were endlessly friendly and helpful. Living in such close proximity to the Prince of Orange's Court, the exiles had a constant stream of visitors like their old friend Sir Dudley Carleton, now James VI and I's ambassador at The Hague. Elizabeth was always given precedence as first lady at the Prince of Orange's Court, and there were invitations to banquets, plays and masques. A diverting trip to Amsterdam was paid for by the States-General and, knowing his guests' love of hunting, Prince Maurice lent them lodgings at Rhenen.

Frederick was an object of curiosity and some pity, but his wife had become an icon for the beleaguered Protestants. Her enemies compared her to Helen, who had caused the Trojan War, saying that she had started the Thirty Years' War, but her many admirers were passionate in their support of her. They could hardly look to Frederick as a source of inspiration, but they declared themselves eager to fight on behalf of this dispossessed

PLATE 44
Frederick and Elizabeth of Bohemia out riding, by Adriaen van de Venne
Rijksmuseum, Amsterdam

Protestant princess who had shown such grace and such undaunted spirit in the face of adversity. Her cousin Christian of Brunswick wore her glove on his helmet, as a medieval champion would have done, and to her horror lost his left arm in her cause.

From both Britain and Germany there were constant requests for her portrait. Michael van Mierevelt painted her many times, sometimes full-length, sometimes head and shoulders only, now with a feather in her hair, now with a spreading lace collar. One particularly beautiful painting shows her with her hair flowing loose, her elaborately embroidered jacket scarcely concealing the fact that she is pregnant. It was probably painted for Frederick himself. Gerard van Honthorst, another famous artist at the Prince of Orange's Court, painted several enormous allegorical groups of the family, as well as providing individual likenesses of them.

Paintings and engravings of Frederick and Elizabeth were to be found hanging in many of the great houses in Britain and the continent, and personal mementoes were treasured too. When Colonel Alexander Cunningham's Will was confirmed in Edinburgh in 1646, it listed among his possessions a gold box with the King of Bohemia's portrait on one side and Elizabeth's on the other, silver basins with the Queen of Bohemia's coat of arms 'in the middle', and a locket containing some of Elizabeth's hair.

As the conflict raged on, ravaging Germany with unprecedented horrors, Frederick spent long periods with his army, enlisting the assistance of first one mercenary general and then another in his attempt to win back the Palatinate, seeing his soldiers slaughtered, striving desperately to find the money for more men and having his hopes dashed time and time again. The States-General had already voted him 10,000 guilders a month for the upkeep of his family, and James VI and I was sending Elizabeth an allowance of £1000 a month with another £500 for Frederick. Elizabeth pawned and sold many of her fabulous jewels, and by 1624 her father had contributed no less than £500,000 to the Protestant cause. Parliament then voted £240,000 a year should be sent, but all too soon it was spent.

Back at the Wassenaer Hof after each failed expedition Frederick was deeply despondent. Accustomed to the wooded hills of Germany, his own splendid castle and its beautiful terraced garden overlooking the Neckar Valley, he disliked the neat brick houses, the flat Dutch landscape, the still waters of the Vijveberg and the crowded streets of The Hague. Weighed down with guilt about the Battle of the White Mountain and the torture and execution of his supporters in Bohemia, he sought solace in Elizabeth's company and it took all her natural optimism to encourage him. If only he had been happy, she could have been perfectly content, enjoying the intrigues and flirtations of her household, going out sightseeing,

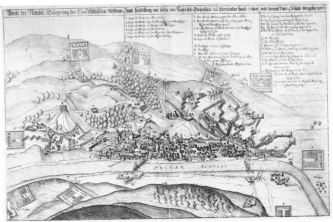

watching masques, tournaments and firework displays, laughing at her ladies' gossip and finding husbands for them. As it was, she strove to comfort him with cheerful advice and find agreeable distractions, planning a trip to see a group of English actors perform *The Scornful Lady* on one occasion, 'to pass the time a little to the King'.

On a more serious note, she did everything she could to win support for him, writing to everyone she knew who might be able to help. Her once elaborate, italic handwriting became a hasty scrawl, often with blots, words scored out or grains of the sand used as blotting paper adhering to the page. The regal flourishes round her signature were still there, but they give an impression of agitation rather than dignity. She had long since abandoned the careful, formal phrases of her childhood letters. Like her father, she loved to tease and, determined to keep up appearances, she sent messages full of nicknames and high-spirited jokes. A letter to Sir Thomas Roe, ends with the words, 'Honest fat body, be assured that you have not a better or truer friend than, Your constant friend, Elizabeth', while the Earl of Carlisle is told, 'I have ever found you so true a friend to me on all occasions as binds me ever to be, honest, worthy Camel's Face, your constant affectionate friend, Elizabeth.' Only occasionally is there a glimpse of

OPPOSITE:
PLATE 45
Frederick, King of Bohemia, during his years of exile, by Gerard van Honthorst
Duke of Buccleuch and Queensberry KT

PLATE 46
The Fall of Heidelberg, 1622, by an unknown engraver
British Museum, London

RIGHT:
PLATE 47
Sir Thomas Roe, diplomat, traveller and faithful supporter of Elizabeth, after Michael van Mierevelt
National Portrait Gallery
London

tiredness and despair as she contemplated the future for her beloved husband and their ever-growing family.

She was pregnant when she arrived in The Hague, and her sixth child was a daughter. Frederick always allowed her to choose the children's names, and she selected Louise Hollandine, as a tribute to her mother-in-law and to the States-General. More children followed in rapid succession: Louis in 1623, Edward in 1625, Henrietta Maria in 1626, Philip in 1627, Charlotte in 1628, Sophia in 1630 and Gustavus Adolphus in 1632. There was no room in the Wassenaer Hof for a royal nursery, and so the Prince of Orange kindly offered a house for the children in the healthier air of Leiden. Frederick's old governess Madame de Plessen and her husband were installed there to look after them and supervise their education. Charles Louis, Elizabeth and Maurice were for the time being left in Berlin, where

PLATE 48
Frederick, Elizabeth and their six eldest children,
Frederick Henry, Charles Louis, Elizabeth, Rupert (Robertus), Maurice and the baby, Louise
Hollandine, about 1622, by an unknown engraver
Scottish National Portrait Gallery

74

PLATE 49
The four eldest children of Frederick and Elizabeth of Bohemia,
Princess Elizabeth, Prince Rupert, Prince Maurice and Prince Charles Louis
by Gerard van Honthorst, 1631
Lent by Her Majesty The Queen

they were happily settled with their grandmother in their aunt and uncle's household, but in 1625 Charles Louis was brought to Leiden to join the others and Elizabeth and Maurice followed three years later.

Three of Elizabeth's children died young. Her fourth son, Louis, 'the prettiest child I ever had', was always delicate. He fell ill when he was almost two, and Elizabeth had him brought back to The Hague, but he died on Christmas Day 1624. Charlotte did not survive infancy and little Gustavus Adolphus, who was epileptic, suffered a long and painful

75

unspecified illness before his death at the age of nine. The others, however, were energetic and healthy. The daughters were carefully educated to be royal brides, while the sons attended Leiden University before being sent for military training. As soon as they were old enough, they would have to fight alongside their father for his inheritance.

In 1625, James VI and I died. 'You may easily judge what an affliction it was to me to understand the evil news of the loss of so loving a father as his late Majesty was to me', Elizabeth wrote to Lord Conway. 'It would be much more but that God hath left me so dear and loving a brother as the King is to me, in whom, next God, I have now all my confidence.' Charles I inherited a debt of over a million pounds from his father, but continued to send money to Frederick and Elizabeth, both for military purposes and for the upkeep of the their household. That same year, Prince Maurice also died, leaving Elizabeth some of his shares in the West Indies Company, as a token of his esteem for her.

His successor was his half-brother, Prince Frederick Henry, whom Elizabeth knew well. Plump, cheerful and kind-hearted, he was not only a

PLATE 50
Frederick Henry,
Prince of Orange by studio of
Sir Anthony van Dyck, a version of
the painting in The Prado
National Trust for Scotland,
Brodick Castle

PLATE 51
Amalia von Solms,
Elizabeth's lady-in-waiting, and
then wife of Frederick Henry, Prince
of Orange, by Michael van
Mierevelt, 1627
Private Collection

highly successful general but also an experienced diplomat. He had been in London in 1603, to congratulate James VI on his accession to the English throne, and he was back in 1613 to attend Elizabeth's wedding. In the spring of 1625 he was himself still unmarried. Prince Maurice, terminally ill, told him that unless he took a wife he would be disinherited. For the past three years, Elizabeth had been encouraging a romance between Frederick Henry and Amalia von Solms, and on 2 April 1625 they were married.

Two days later, Prince Maurice died and Frederick Henry and Amalia were transformed into the new Prince and Princess of Orange. Elizabeth

PLATE 52
Prince Frederick Henry, Elizabeth of Bohemia's eldest son, by Michael van Mierevelt
Hamilton Collection, Lennoxlove House

remained friends with her former lady-in-waiting, acted as godmother to Amalia's first son, and continued to be treated with great deference because of her royal status even though Holland now had its own first lady. The two families shared outings, attended the Kloosterkerke together and enjoyed all manner of entertainments. As the years went by, however, Amalia became notoriously imperious and it took all the combined tact of Elizabeth and Frederick Henry to preserve peaceful relations.

In 1629, Elizabeth's eldest son, Prince Frederick Henry, completed his education and it was arranged that he would join the Prince of Orange's army the following spring. He therefore returned from Leiden to spend

PLATE 53

Elizabeth of Bohemia, painted in The Hague about 1628, by Michael van Mierevelt
Scottish National Portrait Gallery

some time with his parents in The Hague. Elizabeth was recovering from the birth of Princess Charlotte, but she and Frederick were much taken up with the news that the West India Company vessel had captured Spanish galleons laden with gold plate worth £870,000 as well as the Brazilian fleet with a valuable cargo of sugar. Because of the shares Elizabeth had inherited from Prince Maurice, she was entitled to an eighth of the prize money.

The vessels were moored in the Zuyder Zee, and Prince Frederick Henry persuaded his father that they should go to see them. They travelled to Haarlem, had dinner, and hired a boat to take them to Amsterdam. The vessel was overcrowded, and so many other boats were making the same journey that progress was slow. They had left in the early afternoon, but darkness was falling by the time they neared Amsterdam, and with it came a thick fog and a heavy frost. Suddenly, a large cargo vessel loomed out of the mist, there was a violent collision and the passengers on the hired boat were thrown into the icy waters.

In those desperate moments, Frederick heard his son's voice calling, 'Help! Help, Father!', but he could not find him. One of the sailors from the hired boat managed to swim to the cargo vessel and shouted to the crew that the King of Bohemia was in the water. At once they threw a rope to him, and Frederick was saved, soaking, half-frozen, badly bruised and distraught with anxiety about his son. He insisted on the cargo vessel returning three times that night to search for the boy, but it was not until daylight that Prince Frederick was found. He had become entangled in the rigging of the hired boat, and his body was frozen to the mast. When they brought her the news, Elizabeth was so shocked that her anxious household feared that she, too, would die. However, the thought of her husband and his need for her, greater than ever now, was enough to revive her. Frederick Henry was buried privately in the Kloosterkerke, close by the Wassenaer Hof.

When spring came, Elizabeth and Frederick went to Rhenen. They were so fond of it that the previous year Frederick had decided to buy property there. He had accordingly purchased the unoccupied convent of

St Agnes, and they found some consolation in making plans for it. In 1631 work began to convert it into a suitable royal residence. Under the supervision of Bartholomeus van Bassen, the well-known artist, materials from the old convent were used to construct a two-storey building with a large garden behind it. The States of Utrecht generously paid for some of the furnishings. Elizabeth slept in a blue canopied bed with flowered curtains, and her cabinet was hung with blue and brown Spanish leather. Throughout the house there were tapestries on the walls, with typical biblical, mythological and hunting scenes, and there was even a special billiards room.

That summer, Frederick was feeling more optimistic than he had done for many years. Gustavus Adolphus, the King of Sweden, champion of the Protestant cause, had invaded Germany the previous year and had won a series of notable victories. When he captured Mainz, Frederick sent him a

PLATE 54

Elizabeth and the Prince and Princess of Orange playing billiards by Adrian van de Venne, 1626:
Elizabeth is on the left, Amalia van Solms and her husband on the right,
from an album of watercolours that was almost certainly a gift from Prince Henry Frederick
to Elizabeth and her husband

British Museum, London

message of congratulation, and as a result was invited to join the campaign. Convinced that, with Gustavus's help, he could win back the Palatinate at last, he persuaded the Prince of Orange and the States-General to supply him with 17,000 guilders to finance his expedition. It was then that Elizabeth, in gratitude and hope, called her delicate thirteenth child Gustavus Adolphus.

The baby was christened on 13 January 1632, with William, Lord Craven, as his godfather. An amusing little man, Lord Craven was utterly devoted to Elizabeth and his wealth was to help her out of many a financial difficulty. At the age of twelve he had inherited an enormous fortune from his father, a former Lord Mayor of London, but he had recently been serving in the army of the Prince of Orange. He had become a frequent visitor to the Wassenaer Hof, and to Leiden, too, where the young princes and princesses treated him as a favourite uncle. Now, he was going to serve with Frederick in his latest expedition. So was one of Elizabeth's Scottish correspondents, James, 3rd Marquis of Hamilton. A close friend of Charles I, he was joining Gustavus's army with 6000 English and 1000 Scottish soldiers. A few days later, Frederick set off at the head of 2500 Dutch soldiers for the King of Sweden's camp at Frankfurt.

When he arrived, Gustavus treated him with great courtesy, but made no sign of setting off to recapture Heidelberg as Frederick was hoping that he would do. Disillusioned and resentful, Frederick asked permission to leave again, and went to visit the Palatinate. It was a harrowing experience, for the countryside was devastated, and many of the houses and castles were in ruins. Meanwhile, after months of frustrating inactivity, Gustavus marched into Swabia to try to provoke the enemy into action. On 6 November 1632 he finally encountered Count Wallenstein and the imperial army at Lützen. The Protestant forces won a triumphant victory,

PLATE 57
James, 3rd Marquis and later 1st Duke of Hamilton,
friend of Frederick and Elizabeth, by Daniel Mytens, 1629
Scottish National Portrait Gallery

but that day brought disaster, for Gustavus Adolphus himself was killed.

Frederick was at Mainz when he heard the news, suffering from a bout of fever. His health had never been good since the death of his eldest son, and his physician, Dr Christian Rumph, had been privately predicting that he was unlikely to live much longer. Although horrified at the Swedish King's death, he clung to the fact that the Protestant forces had won a decisive victory, and wrote to tell Elizabeth that he was coming to take her back to Germany. On 15 November he assured his household that he was much better, apart from a painful swelling on his neck. The very next day,

PLATE 58
Frederick of Bohemia, near the end of his life, attributed to J.A. van Ravestyn
Private Collection

86

however, he became delirious. The Landgrave of Hesse Darmstadt's chief physician, hastily summoned, diagnosed the plague.

When he knew that he was dying, Frederick sent messages to his children, telling them that they must remain faithful to the Protestant cause and be obedient to their mother. He knew, he said, that Charles I, the Prince of Orange and the States-General would look after Elizabeth, who had ever been the dearest object of his existence. At seven o'clock on the morning of 19 November 1632 he died very peacefully. Dr Rumph set out at once for The Hague to break the terrible news to Elizabeth and found her sitting for her portrait to Michael van Mierevelt. She later said, 'Though Dr Rumph told it me very discreetly, it was the first time that ever I was frighted.' Five months later, she described her shock to her old friend Sir Thomas Roe. She had felt 'as cold as ice, and could neither cry, nor speak, nor eat, nor drink, nor sleep for three days.' She lay in bed for almost a week, 'not being able to do otherwise', and then she got up and put on the black she would wear for the rest of her life.

PLATE 59

Elizabeth of Bohemia, miniature painted by Alexander Cooper
from a portrait by Gerard van Honthorst, about 1632
Private Collection, by courtesy of the Weiss Gallery, London

PLATE 60
Elizabeth of Bohemia as a widow, in 1634, by Gerard van Honthorst
Duke of Buccleuch and Queensberry ᴋᴛ

CHAPTER SIX

The Widow

On 14 December 1632, almost a month after Frederick's death, Elizabeth wrote to Charles I to thank him for his two affectionate letters. 'They found me the most wretched creature that ever lived in the world. And this I shall ever be, having lost the best friend I ever had, in whom was all my delight, having fixed my affections so entirely upon him that I should long to be where he is were it not his children would be left utterly destitute.' As she explained to Sir Thomas Roe, she would grieve for Frederick 'for as long as I live. Though I make a good show in company, yet can I never have any more contentment in this world. For God knows, I had none but I took in his company, and he did the same in mine.'

Charles invited Elizabeth to return to Britain, but she decided to stay where she was. 'I must prefer the welfare of my poor children to my own satisfaction.' Her ten surviving sons and daughters were all under the age of fifteen, the youngest not a year old. Above all else, she must help Charles Louis to continue his father's campaign. It was not simply that he was her favourite son. He was now the rightful Elector Palatine, and for the sake of Frederick's reputation as well as his own, he must win back his inheritance. She was under no illusions about the difficulties involved. Even after the victory at Lützen, the military struggle would have to go on. 'Indeed', she told Archbishop Laud, 'I do not think he will be restored fully, otherwise than by arms. 16 years experience makes me believe it', adding a few weeks later, 'All I fear is that you will think I have too warring a mind for my sex. But the necessity of my fortune has made it [so].' Honthorst painted a new, large portrait group, showing her arriving with her family at the Gates of Paradise, where Frederick and their eldest son were waiting to greet her, and individual portraits of her, although still regal, show her dressed in black, gazing yearningly into the distance.

In 1635, she sent eighteen-year-old Charles Louis to England to ask King Charles for help. Three months later, she allowed his younger brother Rupert to join him. He made a better impression than the reserved, somewhat chilly Charles Louis and eventually their uncle agreed to provide them with a fleet so that they could invade the Lower Palatinate. Lord Craven immediately contributed ten thousand pounds and told Elizabeth that he would go with them to keep an eye on them, but the expedition was a disaster. They were defeated at Vlotho on the banks of the Weser, on 17 October 1638. Charles Louis was hustled from the field by

PLATE 61

Frederick of Bohemia, a posthumous engraving, 1633, by William Hondius after Michael van Mierevelt

Scottish National Portrait Gallery

PLATE 62

Elizabeth of Bohemia, 1630, engraved by William Hondius after Michael van Mierevelt

Scottish National Portrait Gallery

PLATE 63
Prince Rupert of the Rhine, Elizabeth's third son, after Gerard van Honthorst
Blair Castle Collection, Perthshire

his attendants, but Rupert was taken prisoner, as was Lord Craven, who was seriously wounded. He was set free soon afterwards, but it was three years before Rupert was released.

By that time, there was no chance of Charles I giving any further assistance, for Britain had been plunged into Civil War. Elizabeth's two eldest boys travelled to England once more where, to her chagrin, Charles Louis supported parliament instead of his uncle, whom he blamed for not giving him more assistance. Although Prince Rupert of the Rhine earned himself a glamorous reputation as one of the cavalry commanders in the royal army, his mother remained uneasy because she knew how reckless he was. 'I know his disposition is good', she had once told Sir Thomas Roe, 'and he never did disobey me at any time, though to others he was stubborn and wilful ...'

On the advice of Charles Louis, Elizabeth maintained a pretence of neutrality throughout the Civil War, in the hope that parliament would continue to pay the family their pensions. There was little doubt where her real loyalties lay, of course, and she kept an anxious watch on the progress of her brother's cause by means of messengers and correspondence. In 1642 she was able to hear news at first hand when Henrietta Maria, his Queen arrived in Holland with her ten-year-old daughter, Mary, who had just been married to the Prince of Orange's heir. Henrietta stayed for almost a year, trying to pawn some of the English crown jewels to raise money for Charles I's cause. Tall, easy-going Elizabeth had little in com-

PLATE 64
Medal commemorating the marriage of Elizabeth's niece, Princess Mary to Frederick Henry's son, William, Prince of Orange, 1641
Scottish National Portrait Gallery

PLATE 65
Queen Henrietta Maria, Elizabeth's sister-in-law, after a painting by Sir Anthony van Dyck
Scottish National Portrait Gallery

PLATE 66
The Execution of Charles I by an unknown artist
Lord Dalmeny, on loan to the Scottish National Portrait Gallery

mon with her tiny, effervescent, Roman Catholic sister-in-law, but when Henrietta finally sailed back to England, Elizabeth took a protective interest in her small, gloomy daughter.

The two were brought even closer with the dreadful news of the execution of Charles I in 1649. Elizabeth immediately abandoned any pretence of impartiality, and her subsequent references to Oliver Cromwell were full of loathing. 'Sure, Cromwell is the beast in the Revelation, that all kings and nations do worship', she told Sir Edward Nicholas in one of her many letters home. 'I wish him the like end, and speedily.' A year after that there was more sorrow when Mary's young husband died unexpectedly, leaving her to bear his posthumous son a few days later. She called him William, after his father, and from then onwards she and Elizabeth were constantly in each other's company.

It was some consolation that the exigencies of Civil War brought a tide of exiles to the continent, not least Charles I's sons, the young Charles II, James, Duke of York and Henry, Duke of Gloucester. Elizabeth was delighted when they visited her, became very fond of them, and in particular she and Charles shared a close affinity.

93

She saw them all too infrequently, but a procession of royalist supporters visited her Court and found her very well informed about what was
happening in both Scotland and England. One of the first to come was
James, Marquis of Montrose, who arrived in the spring of 1649 and soon
became a particular favourite. 'Wicked Jamie Graham', as she jokingly
called him, had served with her son Maurice during the Civil War. The
dashing Montrose had been a great rival of the more cautious Marquis of
Hamilton, but her old friend Hamilton was dead now, executed on the
same scaffold at Whitehall just three weeks after Charles I himself. She
befriended Montrose without reserve and even thought of marrying him
to her daughter Sophia. Nothing came of the match, however, and
Montrose himself was beheaded in Edinburgh the following year for his
activities on behalf of the royalist cause.

Meanwhile, European diplomacy rather than British military assistance
won back the inheritance of Elizabeth's eldest son. The Peace of Westphalia which ended the Thirty Years' War in 1648 gave Charles Louis the
Lower Palatinate, although he was not allowed the title of First Elector of

PLATE 67
*Charles I, memorial medal
commemorating his execution in 1649*
Scottish National Portrait Gallery

PLATE 68
*Charles II as Prince of Wales,
depicted at the Battle of Edgehill,
by William Dobson*
Scottish National Portrait Gallery

the Holy Roman Empire, nor did he receive the Upper Palatinate. When he returned to The Hague a few months after his uncle's execution, Elizabeth upbraided him bitterly for his support of parliament and he departed soon afterwards for Heidelberg, taking with him a considerable quantity of furnishings from the Wassenaer Hof.

Heidelberg Castle itself had been so badly damaged that he was at first unable to live in it, and the surrounding area had suffered dreadfully during the long years of conflict. He was determined to restore his property and possessions, and equally determined that his extravagant and impoverished mother should not be a perpetual drain on his finances. He therefore refused her demands for the revenues owed to her from her jointure, and instead suggested that she could save money by coming to live in his household at Heidelberg. She knew that such an arrangement would never work, and there was another complication. Charles Louis had fallen out with Charlotte von Hessen-Cassel, the hot-tempered German princess he had married in 1650 and he had installed another lady, Louise von Degenfeld, in his household.

PLATE 69
*James, Marquis of Montrose, one of Elizabeth's Scottish
friends, attributed to William Dobson*
Scottish National Portrait Gallery

PLATE 70
*Mary, Princess of Orange and her son,
the future William II and III,
medal (obverse and reverse)*
British Museum, London

Elizabeth was mortified. 'Your domestique brouilleries troubles me very much', she was telling him in June 1658. 'You may easily imagine that what has happened cannot be hid though your wife has held her peace and, all things considered, she must have been another patient Grisel, which I hear she is not ... I will deal plainly with you as I am bound by what I am to you, to tell you that your open keeping that wench doth you no small dishonour to all persons of all conditions. If everybody could quit their husbands and wives for their ill humours, there would be no small disorder in the world.' Even so, she ended on a placatory note, 'Take not this plain dealing in ill part, for if you were indifferent to me, I would not do it.' Despite their arguments, they always kept in touch with each other, and Charles Louis's daughter Liselotte was Elizabeth's favourite grandchild.

Her younger sons were also a source of continual anxiety. Rupert, now Lord Admiral of Charles II's fleet, was at sea, scouring the West Indies in search of prizes, with Maurice as his Vice Admiral. The two were inseparable, until Maurice was lost during a hurricane near the Virgin Islands in 1652. It was several years before Elizabeth gave up hope that he would one day return. Philip, at the age of eighteen, killed his mother's unpopular chief equerry during an argument on the street, and fled. He became a mercenary, and died in a skirmish in the Ardennes when he was twenty-three. Edward affronted his mother by secretly marrying the Roman Catholic daughter of a French Duke. However, they were soon reconciled.

PLATE 71

Charles Louis, Elector Palatine, Elizabeth's eldest surviving son, from the studio of Sir Anthony van Dyck
National Gallery, London

PLATE 72

Charles Louis and Charlotte of Hesse Cassel, a betrothal medal of 1649
British Museum, London

PLATE 73
Elizabeth of Bohemia in 1650,
by Gerard van Honthorst

Ashdown House,
The Craven Collection,
National Trust

PLATE 74
Prince Edward,
Elizabeth's sixth son
by Gerard van
Honthorst

Marquis of Lothian

CLOCKWISE FROM ABOVE

PLATE 75

Princess Elizabeth, Elizabeth's eldest daughter, after or studio of Gerard van Honthorst

Ashdown House, The Craven Collection, National Trust

PLATE 76

Princess Louise Hollandine, Elizabeth's second daughter, by Gerard van Honthorst

Blair Castle Collection, Perthshire

PLATE 77

Princess Sophia, Elizabeth's youngest daughter, and the mother of George I, by Gerard van Honthorst, 1650

Ashdown House, The Craven Collection, National Trust

Elizabeth's daughters were also a worry. As children of a reigning King of Bohemia, they would have had eligible suitors eagerly competing to marry them, but as penniless exiles they were ignored. Nor did the girls themselves help. Intellectual, absent-minded Elizabeth was preoccupied with astronomy, mathematics and her long correspondence with the celebrated philosopher Descartes, who said that she had one of the most remarkable minds in Europe. Artistic Louise, probably taught by Honthorst, cared only for painting pictures and eventually scandalised Elizabeth by running away to become a Roman Catholic nun in France. She spent the rest of her long life there, happily adorning her convent with her religious paintings.

When Charles Louis was restored to the Lower Palatinate, he decided that he must find husbands for his two younger sisters, who were still of marriageable age. Pretty, pink-cheeked Henrietta Maria, who loved

PLATE 78

Charles II, Elizabeth's nephew, painted during his exile by Gerard van Honthorst, about 1648
Ashdown House, The Craven Collection, National Trust

needlework and domesticity, became the bride of Prince Sigismund Rakoczy von Siebenbürgen in 1651. The Prince and she were delighted with each other, but their brief married life ended a few months later when she died, probably of tuberculosis. Finally, clever, sharp-tongued, amusing Sophia became the wife of Duke Ernest Augustus of Brunswick-Lüneburg. She was at first intended for his brother, but the change of partner did not trouble her. 'I being resolved to love him was delighted to find how amiable he was', she said.

Throughout the 1650s, Elizabeth led an outwardly peaceful life, riding, hunting, going to masques and banquets with Princess Mary, and charming her creditors into allowing her to run up still more debts. She had pawned almost all her jewels, and she owed more than 930,000 guilders. Her generosity was famous, and even her husband had once told her reproachfully, 'I know your ways. You can never refuse anybody anything'. The monthly allowance of 1,000 guilders granted to her by the States General in 1655 did little to help and her letters to Charles Louis became a catalogue of complaints about velvet hangings so rotten that they could not be used, lack of fuel, bread, beer, meat and candles, and the sad state of Rhenen, which was going to rack and ruin. 'I cannot live upon the air', she told her unsympathetic son.

In the midst of these practical difficulties, she remained preoccupied with events in Britain, longing for the restoration of her nephew Charles II. Sometimes their hopes were raised, only to be dashed again, but in May 1659 his prospects improved dramatically. Cromwell was dead now, and his son Richard had just resigned as Lord Protector. In a mood of high excitement, Elizabeth decided to go to Brussels incognito, 'having not seen the King these nine years.' It was a delightful interlude, for he and his brothers made her very welcome, took her about, and endlessly discussed their hopes for the future. The following spring, she was able to tell Charles Louis that the people of London were making great bonfires in the street and drinking to Charles II and his happy return. By mid-April, 'The business in England grows better and better for the King'. Parliament had been dissolved, sequestered lands were to be returned to their owners, and so 'my Lord Craven shall have his again.' Finally, in June, Charles was invited to return to London.

Elizabeth accompanied him to Scheveningen, and attended the celebratory banquet on board the *Royal Charles*. While he then set sail, she made her way back to the shore by barge, with his promise that she would be invited to England and that parliament would pay all her debts. In the ensuing months all his family gathered in London: his brothers James and Henry, his sister Mary and eventually his mother Henrietta Maria with her youngest daughter Minette. Lord Craven went as well, to look after Elizabeth's interests, and she began to feel that she was missing all the excitement. Surely Charles would send for her as soon as his coronation was over. She appreciated that her attendance would have cost him a good deal of money, so she resigned herself to waiting, and in the meantime she received distressing news from London. Her nephew Henry had died in a smallpox epidemic. Worse was to follow, for Mary also fell ill and died on Christmas Eve. Elizabeth went tearfully to Leyden to break the news to the Princess's small son, the future William III.

Restless and unhappy, she thought at first that she might move to the Palatinate, but she and Charles Louis could not agree over the financial arrangements and she felt a deep longing to see her own country again. Moreover, if she were in London she could make sure that parliament granted her an annual allowance. When Lord Craven offered to lend her his own house in Drury Lane, she told her ladies to pack up her things and prepare for the journey.

In fact, Charles did not want her in London because he was engaged in delicate negotiations with the French, to whom she was known to be hostile. However, even the French ambassador in The Hague judged her to be an asset rather than a liability. Reporting her decision to go to England, he commented, 'She talks of returning again to the Hague, but I doubt whether the King, her nephew, will permit her so to do; for assuredly she cannot but be very useful to him, being a good creature, of a temper very

PLATE 79

Princess Mary of Orange, niece of Elizabeth, by Adriaen Hanneman, 1659

Scottish National Portrait Gallery

PLATE 80

William, 1st Earl of Craven, faithful friend and supporter of Elizabeth
probably painted by her daughter Princess Louise, 1647

National Portrait Gallery, London

civil and always equal, one who has never disobliged anybody and who is thus capable, in her own person, of securing affection for the whole royal family and one who, although more than a sexagenarian in age, preserves full vigour of body and mind.' She owed more than 200,000 crowns to a long list of creditors and tradesmen in The Hague, but because of their friendship for her they were allowing her to leave the country without a word of complaint, 'and without any other assurance of their payment than the high opinion they have of her goodness and generosity, and that, as soon as she shall have means to give them satisfaction she will not, although absent and distant, fail to do it.'

The ambassador obligingly agreed to lend her his coach, since her own carriages were already on board the Dutch ships which would take her to Gravesend, and he escorted her to the coast along with her retinue, her daughter Sophia and her husband, Liselotte and a host of Dutch dignitaries. In the midst of the elaborate series of farewells, she received a letter from Charles II telling her to stay where she was. She should not come to London until he sent her an invitation. Horrified, she decided that she could not possibly turn back now. It would be far too embarrassing. She therefore proceeded to Helvoetsluys and sailed for Britain.

Bowing to the inevitable, Charles greeted her with his usual easy affection and she was soon writing proudly to the unappreciative Charles Louis, 'Every week I march to one place or other with the King.' He took her to the opera, to banquets and plays, and she was always welcomed with enthusiasm wherever she went. Thoroughly enjoying herself, she stayed

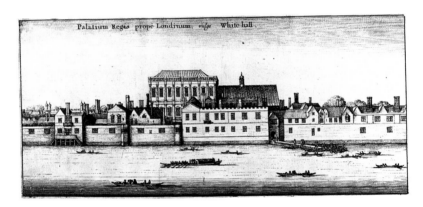

PLATE 81
Whitehall Palace, Charles II's
principal residence. Although Elizabeth did not have
apartments there, she was a frequent visitor
Museum of London

PLATE 82
Medal celebrating the Restoration of Charles II,
Elizabeth's nephew, in 1660
Scottish National Portrait Gallery

PLATE 83
Elizabeth of Bohemia by Gerard van Honthorst, 1642
National Gallery, London

Queen of Bohemia.

on and the following summer arranged to rent the Earl of Leicester's town house. It was currently leased out to the Dutch ambassadors, but as soon as they moved out, she could move in. She therefore sent orders to one of her servants in The Hague to pack up all the decent furnishings in her houses there and at Rhenen. This led to yet another quarrel with Charles Louis, who announced that, as his father's heir, everything belonged to him, and stopped the servants from taking anything away. Mortified at this public airing of their differences, Elizabeth asked Charles II to intervene. He persuaded his cousin to release the furnishings, but even he could not force Charles Louis to pay a larger proportion of the jointure she should have been receiving. He therefore granted her a pension of £12,000 a year himself.

PLATE 84

Anne Hyde, Duchess of York, who was, before her marriage, lady-in-waiting to Princess Mary of Orange and a favourite of Elizabeth, by Sir Peter Lely

Scottish National Portrait Gallery

PLATE 85

James, Duke of York, later James VII and II, Elizabeth's nephew, by Sir Peter Lely

Scottish National Portrait Gallery

On 29 January 1662, she finally moved into Leicester House, but she had been there for only a few days when she fell seriously ill. For some years past she had been troubled with bronchitis in the wintertime, and now she contracted pneumonia. Suffering a pulmonary haemorrhage, she realised that she was near death and sent for the King, the Duke of York and Lord Chancellor Clarendon. She begged them to make sure that all her debts in Holland were paid. They promised to do so, and the King urged her to move to his Palace of Whitehall, where she would be more comfortable. Too weak to comply, she said that she must make her will. Charles Louis was her official heir, of course, but she wanted to make several bequests. Some of her few remaining jewels were to be distributed among her children as mementoes, and the rest were to be given to Prince Rupert. Her faithful friend, Lord Craven, was to have all her pictures and her family papers.

Rupert was with her when she died, propped up in her chair, in the early morning of 13 February 1662. When he heard the news, the Earl of Leicester wrote to tell his friend the Earl of Northumberland, 'My royal tenant is departed. It seems the fates did not think it fit that I should have the honour, which indeed I never much desired, to be the landlord of a Queen. It is a pity that she lived not a few hours more to die upon her wedding day, and that there is not as good a poet to make her epitaph as Dr Donne, who wrote her epithalamium upon that day unto St Valentine.'

She was buried in Westminster Abbey on the evening of 17 February, beside her brother Prince Henry, as was her wish. Nearly fifty years had passed since he had died and she had set off on the long journey that was to take her to Heidelberg, Prague, Berlin and four decades of exile in The Hague. She has been reviled by her critics, then and now, for her extravagance and her apparent preoccupation with idle pleasure. Her admirers have idealised her, using the once scornful terms 'The Queen of Hearts' and 'The Winter Queen' as titles of affectionate respect. Those who knew her were captivated by her charm, her honesty and her good humour. Moreover, she is not only one of the most romantic figures of the seventeenth century. She was the crucial dynastic link between the Stewart monarchy and the royal House of Hanover. In 1716 her grandson, Sophia's son, became King George I and her descendants have occupied the throne of Britain ever since.

PLATE 86
George I, Elizabeth's grandson, by Sir Godfrey Kneller
Duke of Roxburghe

THE HOUSES OF
STEWART AND HANOVER

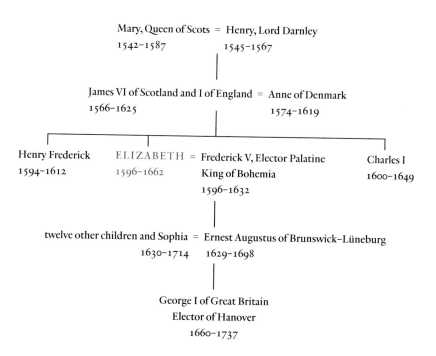

Mary, Queen of Scots = Henry, Lord Darnley
1542-1587   1545-1567

James VI of Scotland and I of England = Anne of Denmark
1566-1625   1574-1619

Henry Frederick   ELIZABETH = Frederick V, Elector Palatine   Charles I
1594-1612   1596-1662   King of Bohemia   1600-1649
                                   1596-1632

twelve other children and Sophia = Ernest Augustus of Brunswick–Lüneburg
                    1630-1714   1629-1698

George I of Great Britain
Elector of Hanover
1660-1737

ELIZABETH'S CHILDREN

1   Frederick Henry 1614-1629
2   Charles Louis 1617-1680
3   Elizabeth 1618-1680
4   Rupert of the Rhine 1619-1682
5   Maurice 1620-1652
6   Louise Hollandine 1622-1709
7   Louis 1623-1624
8   Edward 1625-1663
9   Henrietta Maria 1626-1651
10   Philip 1627-1650
11   Charlotte 1628-1631
12   Sophia 1630-1714
13   Gustavus Adolphus 1632-1641

FURTHER READING AND SOURCES

Akrigg, G. P. V. ed., *Letters of King James VI and I*, London,1984

Baker, L. M. ed., *The Letters of Elizabeth, Queen of Bohemia*, London, 1953

Bunnett, F, *Louise Juliane, Electress Palatine*, London, 1862

Caus, S. de, *Hortus Palatinus*, Frankfurt ,1620

England und Kurpfalz, exhibition catalogue, Heidelberg Castle 1963

Gardiner, S. R. , *The Thirty Years' War*, London, 1865–8

Godfrey, A., *A Sister of Prince Rupert*, London, 1909

Gorst-Williams, Jessica, *Elizabeth, The Winter Queen*, London, 1977

Green, Mary Anne Everett, *Elizabeth, Electress Palatine and Queen of Bohemia*, London, 1909

W. H., *True Picture and Relation of Prince Henry*, Leiden, 1634

Hoogsteder, Willem-Jan, 'De Schilderijen van Frederik en Elizabeth, Konig en Koningin van Bohemen', unpublished doctoral thesis, Utrecht, 1986

Keblusek, Marika and Zijlmans, Jori, ed., *Princely Display: The Court of Frederik Hendrik of Orange and Amalia van Solms*, The Hague, 1997

Lewalski, Barbara Kiefer, *Writing Women in Jacobean England*, London, 1993

Marshall, Rosalind K., *Henrietta Maria*, London, 1990

Memoirs of Sophia, Electress of Hanover 1630–80, translated by H. Forester, London, 1888

Nichols, John, *The Progresses, Processions and Magnificent Festivities of King James the First*, 4 vols, London, 1828

Oman, Carola, *Elizabeth of Bohemia*, London, 1938

Plowden, Alison, *The Stuart Princesses*, London, 1996

Ploeg, Peter van der and Vermeeren, Carola ed., *Princely Patrons: The Collection of Frederick Henry of Orange and Amalia of Solms*, The Hague, 1997

Rohr, Alheidis von, '"Peint par Madame l'Abbesse", Louise Hollandine Prinzessin von der Pfalz, 1622–1709' in *Niederdeutsche Beitr,ge zur Kunstgeschichte*, Berlin, 1989

Royalton-Kisch, Martin, *Adriaen van de Venne's Album*, British Museum Publications, 1988

Scarisbrick, Diana, 'Anne of Denmark's Jewellery Inventory' in *Archaeologia*, CIX, 1991, pp.193–244

Scarisbrick, Diana, 'The Winter Queen in Exile' in *Country Life*, 19 March 1992, pp.70–1

Strachan, Michael, *Sir Thomas Roe, 1581–1644: a Life*, London, 1989

Strong, Roy, *Prince Henry Frederick*, London, 1986

The Winter Queen: Elizabeth, Queen of Bohemia and her Family, exhibition catalogue, National Portrait Gallery, London, 1963

Williams, Ethel Carleton, *Anne of Denmark*, London, 1970

Willson, David Harris, *King James VI and I*, London, 1963

MANUSCRIPT SOURCES

Scottish Record Office, Testament of Colonel Alexander Cunningham, 8 October 1646 Edinburgh Commissary Court, CC8/8/62.

Letters of Elizabeth of Bohemia to the Earl of Mar, S.R.O., Mar and Kellie Muniments, GD124/15/57/8

Letters of Elizabeth of Bohemia to the 3rd Marquis of Hamilton, S.R.O., Hamilton Archives, GD406/1/145

PORTRAIT ARCHIVES

Heinz Archive, National Portrait Gallery, London

Portrait Archive, Scottish National Portrait Gallery

Witt Library, Courtauld Institute of Art, London